IT'S ALL ABOUT
THE LAMB

Warren Ravenscroft

It's All About the Lamb
© **Warren Ravenscroft 2024**

Paperback ISBN: 978-0-6486422-7-5
eBook ISBN: 978-0-6486422-8-6

Cover image: Linda Braine

Scripture taken from the New King James Version®.
Copyright © 1982 by Thomas Nelson.
Used by permission. All rights reserved.

All rights reserved. No part of this publication may be reproduced, stored in a retrieval system, or transmitted in any form or by any means electronic, mechanical, photocopying, recording, or therwise, without the prior written permission of the author.

Published in Australia by Warren Ravenscroft
www.wittonbooks.com

A catalogue record for this book is available from the National Library of Australia

> *"Do not think that I came to destroy
> the Law or the Prophets.
> I did not come to destroy but to fulfil.
> For assuredly, I say to you,
> till heaven and earth pass away,
> one jot or one tittle will by no means pass
> from the law till all is fulfilled."*
>
> Matthew 5:17–18

Contents

Introduction	7
PART 1: The Passover	**15**
Egypt	17
Sinai	23
Jericho	29
Centralised Worship	41
Jesus, the Passover Lamb	59
The Passover Replaced	83
Observance of Passover Today	103
Marriage Supper of the Lamb	119
PART 2: The Journey of the Tabernacle	**129**
The Tabernacle of Meeting	131
The Tabernacle of the Lord	137
The Tabernacle's Journey in the Promised Land	153

PART 3: The Journey of the Ark of the Covenant   165

The Ark of the Covenant 167

PART 4: It's All About the Lamb   185

Alpha and Omega 187
Poem by Dr Richard Booker, "The Shaking" 210

CHARTS

Kings of Israel 48
First Temple Timeline 56
Ancestry of Two Blessed Families 60
Trials of Jesus and Outcome 70
Old Covenant Law, New Covenant Grace 79
Old Covenant, New Covenant 82
The Timeline of Paul's Ministry 90
Second Temple Timeline 101

Construction of the Tabernacle 140
The Children of Israel on the March 146
Tabernacle Camps 149

The Journey of the Ark of Testimony 182
The Journey of the Ark of the Covenant 184

Other books by the Author 213

Introduction

The Path of Life, published previously, dealt with the three promises given to Abram. This book, 'It's All About the Lamb', is both a companion book and a stand-alone book, as it deals with the Passover as the preparation for the escape from Egypt and its development across the centuries to the present day. It also discusses the Tabernacle and the Ark of the Covenant as foreshadowing symbols of Jesus' ministry.

As all scripture is divinely inspired, the central theme from Genesis to Revelation is all about Jesus and the revealed plan Father God had for His Son. Jesus is revealed in three different ways through the thoughts written in this book.

First, there is The Passover and the recorded ways they changed over the many years. Secondly, the Tabernacle Journey explores the often-hidden secrets that are contained within the Word of God to those who would try, with the Holy Spirit's guidance, to secure for themselves many rare gems selected especially for themselves.

Thirdly, Jesus is revealed through the Ark of Testimony or the Ark of the Covenant, as the presence of Father God, who accompanies and dwells in the secret place of the Most High, explains a story all of its own, although most of its journey is associated with the Tabernacle.

The Passover had changed over the years from what was a basic meal in Egypt to what is celebrated today. As the first Passover was the introduction to the covering and protection the Lord provided to His chosen people, the other Passovers recorded in scripture changed over time until what is now celebrated is an elaborate version of the celebration in Biblical times.

They should have appreciated and understood what Father God had provided for their salvation and freedom. However, through disobedience, grumbling and failure to comply with the Lord's will, they forfeited Grace, which would have taken them eventually to the real Promised Land.

When settled in Canaan and obeying the Laws of the Lord, the Hebrews had arrived in the physical promised land. However, the spiritual promised land is the New Jerusalem, granted by Grace as an eternal inheritance and reserved for those who persevered and accepted without grumbling and disobedience.

The First Passover consisted of a male lamb of the first year without blemish, separated for four days, killed at twilight, and roasted whole in the fire, not boiled or eaten raw. The accompaniment to the meal was unleavened bread and bitter herbs. Some of the blood from the slain lamb was applied to the doorposts and the lentil with hyssop.

Introduction

Any of the left-over lamb was to be burnt in the fire before morning. The Israelites were dressed to travel as they ate the meal in haste with a belt on their waist, sandals on their feet, and a staff in their hand. They were not to leave the confines of the house they were in under any circumstance.

The Second Passover was ordained by the Lord in the second year after the children of Israel had left Egypt and was celebrated in the camp at Saini after the building and the completion of the Tabernacle. The question to be asked is, "How was the second Passover celebration different to the first?" To answer this question, the Levitical Law given by Father God, along with the Ten Commandments, need to be explored.

The Third Passover recorded occurred some forty-three years after leaving Egypt. Much had happened in the in-between as about three years had passed, and while the children of Israel were camped at Kadesh Barnea, disobedience proved a stumbling block for all those twenty years of age and over who came out of Egypt. An extra forty years was added to their journey, which was the reward for their disobedience, as they never entered the Promised Land they chose to accept but then rejected.

While the Passover and the other feast days were enjoyed, parts that were to be adhered to were lost over the years. Only after the laws had been reinstated after the children of Israel had entered the Promised Land was the Passover observed as the Lord had decreed in some form.

The Fourth Passover entered into a new phase when King Hezekiah instigated central worship in the refurbished Temple in Jerusalem. Instead of a family-centred Passover, the Levites and priests took an active role, which took away the rights of the head of the family to some degree. As this move proved to be a logistical disaster, other parts laid down by the Lord to Moses changed to accommodate the new rules.

The Fifth Passover was recorded when Jesus shared the celebration with His disciples in the upper room. Over time, much had changed as the priests and Levites had so infiltrated the laws and what they now conveyed as acceptable. Passover is a celebration that remembers the escape of the ancient Israelites from Egypt.

Jesus and His disciples were celebrating the Passover meal together, but as this was the last meal Jesus would share with His disciples, He took elements of the Passover meal and made them symbolic of His impending death. Jesus made a significant addition to the Passover Feast, as He instigated a New Covenant to replace the Old Covenant. Cups of wine had been introduced to the meal as Jesus said:

> *"I say to you,*
> *I will not drink of the fruit of the vine*
> *from now until that day*
> *when I drink it new with you*
> *in My Father's kingdom."*

Matthew 26:29

Introduction

The Passover Replaced retraces the path of the Passover from its origins to today and the many changes that have taken place in its history. The observance and the meaning have also been modified to accommodate a changing culture and need. Much has been lost from the first Passover, whereas the first Passover was Physical and Spiritual, the experience of most traditionalists is that of one focused on works to obtain the spiritual application required.

The Sixth Passover feast that is celebrated today is very different to all the other Passovers. Much has been added through better understanding to Remember, Teach, and be Thankful for what the Lord had accomplished in Egypt, the Desert and the Promised Land.

For the Christian who chooses to celebrate and remember the Passover, Jerusalem, where Jesus suffered and died, but more importantly, been raised to new life, so that the fulness of the Gentiles, through the release of the Holy Spirit took place, allows the Passover to reveal an even greater understanding and appreciation for what Father God accomplished.

The Seventh Passover is reserved for the *'called'* as *'many are called but few are choice'* (Matthew 22:14). When Jesus met with His disciples for the last Passover meal He had on this earth, He prophesied that He would not drink from the fourth cup until He drank it new in His Father's Kingdom. Only those who are found righteous will be invited to attend, unlike the eleven disciples who Jesus assured would be with Him.

The Seventh Passover is the final Passover, which is called *'The Marriage Supper of the Lamb'*, a grand and fitting celebration to be shared with those who have on the garments of Righteousness and Praise. These are supplied to us freely by our Saviour, Jesus Christ, as there is nothing we can do to earn them for ourselves except by accepting His invitation to be His follower, obediently obeying the known will of Father God as He reveals Himself to our heart.

Moving from the Passover to the Tabernacle, which provides the basis for the sacrificial worship to be carried out, many hidden details are revealed which have been concealed. As the Tabernacle travelled through changing people and what was spiritually accepted, good and bad priests kept the way to Father God, often disgracing and offending the Lord, who set the Tabernacle as a place where He was to be worshipped and obeyed.

The Ark of the Covenant reveals a story all of its own that is centred on Father God, as this is the place where the Lord communicated His expressed will to the covenant children and others who would dare to intervene in His affairs.

From Mount Sinai, the birthplace of the Ark of Testimony, to the destruction of Herod's temple, it proved a power to some and a stumbling block to others. God was and is always in control, despite the circumstances, man's wisdom, not the Lord, is proven time and time again to be folly. Only when the Lord's will is obtained and understood will the way ahead be opened to the revealed will of the Spirit.

Introduction

Alpha and Omega, as the title suggests, is the beginning to the ending of all things spiritual, as Jesus is the central core of our spiritual life, or should be, allowing the power of the Holy Spirit to infiltrate our life. Father God always required worship from before the world was created but has been denied on so many levels for so many years, but in the end, He will have His way and a nation of priests to worship Him endlessly in the New Jerusalem.

Part 1

The Passover

Egypt

When Moses was living in exile in Midian, he had an intimate encounter with the Lord at the unconsumed burning bush, where he was told about the plan for the remainder of his life. The Lord had chosen Moses to go back to Egypt and lead the Hebrews out of slavery from under the rule of Pharaoh. After Moses had consented to carry out the Lord's commands, the Lord said:

> *"Then you shall say to Pharaoh,*
> *'Thus says the Lord:*
> *'Israel is My son, My firstborn.*
> *So I say to you,*
> *let My son go that he may serve Me.*
> *But if you refuse to let him go,*
> *indeed I will kill your son, your firstborn'.'"*
>
> Exodus 4:22–23

Moses, along with his older brother Aaron, approached Pharaoh and told him that their God required the Hebrews to go for a three-day journey into the desert and worship Him.

As Pharaoh challenged Moses to his demand, Moses responded with the words the Lord had given him:

> *"Let My people go,*
> *that they may serve Me in the wilderness."*
>
> Exodus 7:16b

Nine plagues had passed, and Pharaoh was unrelenting as Moses knew he would be. Moses met with the elders of each tribe and outlined to them the directions for what would become the Passover meal, an ordinance that would be observed to the Lord for what He was about to accomplish, showing His power over all the gods of Egypt.

The elders passed through the city of Goshen, instigating all that the Lord had told Moses to complete. The meal to be prepared and eaten must have appeared strange to the Hebrews, as nothing like this had ever happened before.

The Israelites had no idea of the spiritual significance the tenth plague would have for them. The first four plagues impacted both the Egyptians and the Hebrews, and the next five had little impact on the Hebrews. However, this tenth plague would impact them both physically and spiritually. For the Hebrews, this tenth plague had a dual focus, which would change their thinking and lives forever. They were to obey the Lord, whose instructions were delivered by Moses, guaranteeing both physical and spiritual protection from impending doom and death.

This was a family event as each family was to slaughter a lamb unless they were too small in number to consume the meat. In this situation, two families could dine together as were their needs. One could have imagined that many grumbled about what was to take place, but without an alternative, they carried out the prescribed meal in preparation and detail.

Each family was to take an unblemished lamb under the age of one year and separate it from the rest for four days. On the 14th day of Nissan, at twilight, the lamb was to be killed, and some of the blood put aside to use later, with the aid of hyssop to apply it on the doorposts and lentil. This was a sign for the Hebrews that they were protected.

The lamb was to be roasted whole, and only the flesh was to be eaten (Exodus 12:8), with unleavened bread and bitter herbs for an accompaniment.

> *"Do not eat it raw,*
> *nor boiled at all with water,*
> *but roasted in fire,*
> *its head with its legs and its entrails."*
>
> Exodus 12:9

The children of Israel were to be fully dressed to travel with a belt around the waist and a rod in their hand, as they must stay together inside the house for the entire evening. No one was to venture outside.

The proceedings must have surprised them as they were required to be obedient to the Lord's known will. However, the Israelites followed the Lord's directions, which provided a covering for them as the Lord moved over the land of Egypt.

As each took a portion of lamb, along with the unleavened bread and some bitter herbs, one could imagine they talked among themselves, as the quietness that prevailed outside would have been eerie as not even a dog's bark was heard.

Around midnight, the stillness of the night was broken by the crying and wailing of the Egyptians as they discovered that their first-born sons had died. Even the cattle groaned at the loss of some of their herd. Moses and Aaron were called to Pharaoh and told to leave with haste, which the Hebrews did, as they burnt any leftovers, gathered a few things to take with them and orderly went out of Goshen, following the direction and lead of Moses.

The Hebrews would long remember this night, which was titled 'Passover', as the Lord passed over all those who were obedient to His directions or commands. This was a new beginning for the children of Israel as they set out on a voyage of discovery. Moses remembered the covenant Joseph had made with the children of Israel, saying:

"God will surely visit you,
and you shall carry up my bones from here."

Genesis 50:25b

Moses honoured the oath and took the bones of Joseph as they finally left to inherit the Promised Land.

To summarise the Egyptian Passover, it was a family event where the head of the family was to supervise the preparation and the meal. The lamb was to be roasted whole, complete, not gutted or any bone broken.

The family or families were to join in one house with blood applied to the doorway and not to venture outside. They were to be fully dressed to travel, as the meal was eaten in haste, anything leftover had to be burnt in the morning.

"Do not eat it raw, nor boiled at all with water." The lamb could not be eaten that way, as the lamb had to remain complete, for it was on the cross that the Lamb of God was to experience the fire of Father God's righteous wrath, a truth we should never forget. We are to delight in the Lamb of God and feed on Him, the Bread of Life.

Sinai

Just over one year had passed since the Hebrews had left Egypt, and the Lord reminded Moses that they should have observed the Passover. The Ten Commandments had been given along with the camping arrangements, but they were not in the Promised Land, as the general thinking was they would have celebrated the Passover in the Promised Land.

The Lord was gradually shaping His chosen children into people who would love and serve Him. Trust was instilled during the first Passover, then protection and provision as they passed through the Red Sea; also, manna and water were supplied in abundance as they travelled His path through the desert.

The Lord had given to Moses His proposed laws for the children of Israel to accept or reject. After agreeing to what the Lord had ordained, Moses was given the Law at Mount Sinai, where the children of Israel were camped and had been for some time.

But the Lord was still refining His called people, as they were numbered in a census and then camped in their tribes as the Lord indicated. Other additions were given to Moses to accompany the Law, as the construction and building of the Tabernacle and the Passover Feast and their observance were outlined.

Moses was instructed to build the Tabernacle and the furnishings as they were His priority, and the Lord instructed Moses to appoint skilled tradespeople to make and construct a visible place for the presence of the Lord to dwell.

The children of Israel were instructed to bring gifts, materials and supplies, but far more was given than required, so Moses told them to stop giving as they had sufficient to complete what the Lord required. Aaron and his sons were consecrated to serve the Lord in priestly duties along with others.

When the Tabernacle was completed, Moses inspected everything and found that the building and furniture were without blemish and acceptable for the Lord to descend and fill the Tabernacle with His presence. All was in place for the Lord to instruct the children of Israel further in their spiritual journey.

"Now the Lord spoke to Moses
in the Wilderness of Sinai,
in the first month of the second year
after they had come out of the land of Egypt, saying:
'Let the children of Israel keep the Passover
at its appointed time'."

Numbers 9:1–2

The Lord had established that the Passover was the first of seven joyous Feasts the children of Israel were to observe over the following years. Three were to be observed now: the Passover, the Feast of Unleavened Bread and the Feast of Firstfruits, as they were a complete feast that lasted seven days. The other four feasts, the Feast of Weeks, the Feast of Trumpets, Yom Kippur, and the Feast of Tabernacles, although observed, held more significance when the present situations experienced and the decisions made in the future became their past. (Exodus 23:14).

The observance of the second Passover was slightly different to the first, as the presence of the Lord was visible to them and, as they were protected, they did not need to apply the blood to the doorway of their tent. Back in Egypt, the blood on the doorposts was a sign for them that the Lord would Passover as they would be protected by the blood of the slain lamb. Exodus 12:13

The Lord had provided laws concerning what could and couldn't be eaten. At the first Passover, only the roasted flesh was to be eaten (Exodus 12:8), now an addition was added when the Lord said:

> *"You shall not eat any fat*
> *or drink the blood,*
> *of ox, sheep, or goat."*
>
> Leviticus 7:22–27

The Feast of Passover extended for seven days as the Hebrews were required to eat unleavened bread to accompany their meal and the following meals. The unleavened bread would have been made from the manna the Lord provided. The second feast, the Feast of Unleavened Bread, was followed by the Feast of Firstfruits, which was part of the Passover Feasts, but the Feast of Firstfruits would not be celebrated until they were settled in the Promised Land. Leviticus 23:10

Passover was a family festive time, as the Israelites joyously remembered how the Lord had delivered them from oppression and slavery to worship Him and obey His laws as He required. While they had faltered and worshipped the golden calf that Aaron carved for them, their continued obedience was what the Lord required. The Law laid out in no uncertain terms what each person of accountable age was to observe and fulfil.

Only now, as the Lord continued to train and guide the children of Israel, Moses was instructed to observe the Passover as the time had been over a year since they left Egypt. Moses carried out the instructions of the Lord and relayed them to the elders from each of the tribes. The people accepted that the feast days were to be regarded as a Sabbath, free from any work, as each day on which a joyous feast occurred was in addition to the other Sabbaths, which were every seven days.

To celebrate the second Passover, the children of Israel remembered what was required in the first Passover so they would have separated the unblemished lamb, under the age of one year, to a place on its own. After four days, which was the fourteenth day of the month, at twilight, the head of the household would kill the lamb and roast the guttered skinned carcass over the fire without breaking any bones.

Unleavened Bread, along with Bitter Herbs, accompanied the meal, and each person was to remain within their tent for the evening:

> *"And you shall roast and eat it*
> *in the place which the Lord your God chooses,*
> *and in the morning,*
> *you shall turn and go to your tents."*
>
> Deuteronomy 16:7

While the Passover was a family event, the Levites carried out the other sacrifices that accompanied each of the feasts. Burnt offerings were to be offered along with grain and drink offerings on the day following Passover. These were carried out within the confines of the Tabernacle. On the seventh day, no work was to be carried out as this was a holy convocation or a day similar to a Sabbath. Although the Sabbath was observed, the sacrifices were not offered until the children of Israel had entered the Promised Land. Numbers 28:16–25

To summarise the Wilderness of Sinai Passover, the blood of protection on the doorway was replaced with the continual presence of the Lord. The flesh of the lamb was the only acceptable part to be served, not fat, blood or entrails. As the Holy Spirit refines us, we are to partake of Jesus as He is the bread of life and feast on His flesh.

Jericho

> "Now the children of Israel camped in Gilgal,
> and kept the Passover on the fourteenth day of the month
> at twilight on the plains of Jericho. And they ate of the produce
> of the land on the day after the Passover, unleavened bread
> and parched grain, on the very same day. Then the manna ceased
> on the day after they had eaten the produce of the land;
> and the children of Israel no longer had manna,
> but they ate the food of the land of Canaan that year."
>
> Joshua 5: 10–12

Forty years had passed since any recorded Passovers were celebrated after Mount Sinai. Apart from Joshua and Caleb, all those who had left Egypt had died in the desert because they disobeyed the Lord's command to go in and take the Promised Land. Miriam, Aaron, and Moses had all joined their ancestors, while Joshua was anointed the leader of the children of Israel, along with Eleazar, the third son of Aaron, as high priest.

Moses had described the seven feasts they were to celebrate throughout the year; however, only two feasts were observed in the wilderness wanderings. While the seven feasts were in place, their real meaning escaped them all, as the significance of each feast only became a reality as the years passed.

The first two feasts were observed: the Passover and the Feast of Unleavened Bread. The observance of the Feast of First Fruits was reserved until the children of Israel had entered the Promised Land, as only when they had produced produce for themselves and the manna withdrawn would they be able to offer what they had obtained from the land the Lord had blessed.

Before the Jordan River was crossed, two and a half tribes had already settled for their inheritance, Reuben and Gad, along with half the tribe of Manasseh. Only after covenanting with Moses for all their fighting men to accompany the other tribes were they allowed to settle south of the Jordan River. At least seven to fourteen years would pass after the crossing of the Jordan River before these fighting men would return home to family and friends.

When the other Israelite tribes were camped at Acacia Grove, the time came for them to cross the Jordan River and move into the promised inheritance given to their ancestor Abram so many years previous. All the kings in Canaan felt secure until the Jordan River dried up and the children of Israel crossed over.

When the kings and subjects witnessed the Israelites crossing the Jordan River on dry land, scripture records that *'The hearts of the kings melted'* (Joshua 5:1b). The new generation of Israelites had experienced for themselves a river crossing and had passed over from the old way of life to the new.

Joshua set up camp in the plains of Jericho at a place called Gilgal when the Lord commanded Joshua to circumcise the sons of Israel (Joshua 5:2). Circumcision began as a sign of the covenant between the Lord and Abraham (Genesis 17:10–14). Its practice, however, had been suspended for over forty years, most likely as another sign of apathy and disobedience to the Law.

This outward sign was meaningless unless coupled with an inward serving of fleshly deeds or circumcision of the heart. Moses had recorded the heartfelt message contained within the Law when he wrote the words of the Father:

> *"And the Lord your God will circumcise your heart*
> *and the heart of your descendants,*
> *to love the Lord your God*
> *with all your heart and with all your soul,*
> *that you may live."*
>
> Deuteronomy 30:6

As the heart of this new generation had a different understanding and appreciation for the way of the Lord, *"Joshua circumcised their sons whom He raised up in their place; for they were uncircumcised, because they had not been circumcised on the way."* Joshua 5:7

Many years would pass before this prophecy would be fulfilled. Ezekiel, when prophesying to the Israelites of his day, wrote the following:

"I will give you a new heart
and a new spirit within you;
I will take the heart of stone out of your flesh
and give you a heart of flesh.
I will put My spirit within you
and cause you to walk in My statues,
and you will keep My judgements
and do them."

Ezekiel 36:26–27

Israel had camped for many months in the plains on the eastern side of the Jordan River, across from Jericho (Numbers 22:1). The Lord could have commanded this mass circumcision then when they were protected from the Canaanites by the barrier of the Jordan River, but instead, the Lord waited until they had crossed the Jordan, and were more vulnerable to the Canaanites, to make their army defenceless. In faith, Israel obeyed as they trusted the Lord to protect them when their fighting men couldn't.

The Israelites celebrated the Passover Feast on the evening of the 14th day of the month when they were camped at Gilgal on the flatlands around Jericho. The day after the Passover, they ate some of the food that was grown in the land. Before we proceed with the Jericho Passover, there is much required to form the foundation before the Passover could be observed.

Worldly wisdom would have called for an immediate attack while the people of the land were disheartened and before they could make last-minute preparations. Instead, the Lord called for a three-day delay as the fighting men stayed in the camp until they were healed, while Israel observed the word of the Lord.

This circumcising was a strange thing for Joshua, a keen military commander, to do, as he incapacitated his whole fighting force, an absolutely unmilitary act. It would appear foolish to march your men right into the heat of the enemy and then disable your fighting force. Joshua did it, nevertheless, because the Lord told him to. This faith would lead to the conquest of Canaan.

As I read that the fighting men required three days for healing, I was prompted to remember the story of Jonah and how it took three days to heal this man in the belly of a prepared fish. I also remember that our Lord was three days between His death and resurrection to enable healing for all those who would find refuge in Him from the sin-filled lives they possessed.

The Passover celebration would have resembled that observed in the wilderness as they repeated what they had observed and completed when they wandered in the wilderness for forty years. The lamb killed between the evenings on the fourteenth, skinned, guttered and roasted, accompanied with unleavened bread and bitter herbs. The story of their predecessors leaving Egypt, along with the plagues and the crossing of the Red Sea, would be remembered as the father of the house shared all the details to ensure the children would remember.

But there was something different about this Passover from those previously partaken. They were camped at Gilgal, and kept the Passover on the fourteenth day of the month at twilight on the plains of Jericho as they ate of the produce of the land on the day after the Passover, unleavened bread and parched grain, on the very same day. While the unleavened bread could have been made from manna, the unleavened bread eaten the following day was made from the produce of the land.

There was a sense of completion in this Passover as the Israelites were no longer in the wilderness but were finally on the fringe of the Promised Land, they had crossed over from the wilderness journey and were now in the land which held a new journey for the faithful. The Feast of the Passover commemorated the great work of redemption the Lord accomplished for Israel in freeing them from slavery in Egypt.

The generation that died in the wilderness was, for this new generation, a reminder of Egypt. They were to have no such connection, by their faith and obedience, they were a Promised Land people, not a slave people, but were:

- A people of God suited for His Promised Land.
- Had been set free from Egypt.
- Knew God was real and put Him first.
- Observed God's commands and His rules.
- They accepted His Lordship.
- Brought order and organisation into their lives.
- Received and practised the Lord's ordinances.
- Trusted the Lord's provision through their hard work.
- Take risks for the Lord.
- Didn't expect lives of ease and comfort.
- Dealt with sin in their midst.
- Conquer as they followed their leader, Joshua.

Were these new people ready for the unexpected as the Lord removed some of their food supply? The manna ceased on the day after they had eaten the produce of the land, as the children of Israel no longer required manna, but they ate the food of the land of Canaan that year. The Lord didn't want Israel to get lazy but to live in a new partnership of trust with Him. The Israelites had trusted the Lord to bring the manna for six out of seven days, but they had also trusted Him to provide through other means. This fulfilled what the Lord had said:

> *"And the children of Israel ate manna forty years,*
> *until they came to an inhabited land;*
> *they ate manna until they came to the border*
> *of the land of Canaan."*
>
> Exodus 16:35

The children of Israel were now fed with the produce of the land, and their future supply would depend on their labour. The Israelites would be as surely fed by the Lord in the land as they had been in the wilderness, but they would now be responsible for co-operation with Him in the labour of their own hands. The Lord never employs supernatural methods of supplying needs that can be met by natural means.

Miracles of the Manna

> *"Then the manna ceased on the day*
> *after they had eaten the produce of the land;*
> *and the children of Israel no longer had manna,*
> *but they ate the food of the land of Canaan that year."*
>
> Joshua 5:12

Manna had been part of their diet since the Lord provided bread for them in the Wilderness of Sin (Exodus 16:4) until the day after the Passover when they were settled into the

Promised Land. When the children of Israel saw what the Lord had provided, they said, "What is this?" or the Hebrew word 'Manna'. Manna was not what they had expected, but was anything the Lord did acceptable to this grumbling, disobedient group of people? Manna is described as *'like a white coriander seed, and the taste was like wafers made with honey'*. Exodus 16:31

The provision of the manna was miraculous, as the Lord instructed the people to only gather sufficient manna as they needed and not to store excess. Some did, and by the next day, it had turned rotten and stunk, so it was discarded. This was the first miracle of the manna. The second was that the manna kept good for the Sabbath as they did not gather on the rest day, as the Lord provided none. Six days, they gathered, and on the seventh, they did not. Exodus 16:23–26

The third miracle was that the Lord provided the manna for over forty years. This proved to be forty years past the Lord's expected number of years to provide because the children of Israel disobeyed and would not go in and conquer the Promised Land. How this act of disobedience changed the outcome for Moses, Miriam, Aaron and all those who came out of Egypt twenty years of age and over.

But there is a fourth miracle that is often overlooked. I share with you the following verses of scripture:

Then Moses said,

"This is the thing which the Lord has commanded:

> *'Fill an omer with it, to be kept for your generations,*
> *that they may see the bread*
> *with which I fed you in the wilderness,*
> *when I brought you out of the land of Egypt'.*
> *And Moses said to Aaron,*
> *'Take a pot and put an omer of manna in it,*
> *and lay it up before the Lord,*
> *to be kept for your generations'.*
> *As the Lord commanded Moses,*
> *so Aaron laid it up before the Testimony,*
> *to be kept."*
>
> Exodus 16:32–34

Aaron deposited a jar of manna in the sanctuary, in the 'Ark of the Covenant', so that future generations would recognise that their ancestors had survived in the wilderness only because of the Lord's providential hand. The Manna was placed in the jar containing the Manna Bread about 1440 BC and remained perfect until somewhere about 590 BC, when Nebuchadnezzar sieged Jerusalem and ransacked Solomon's temple, taking everything as spoil, including many of the Israelites as slaves.

One could imagine that those who ransacked the temple were overcome with all the gold and would not have had any idea of the significance of the two stone tablets, probably written in Hebrew, Aaron's Rod and a Jar containing some bread, so they discarded them as worthless. Bread that usually moulded and stank overnight, kept good and eaten on the Sabbath remained in its unblemished state for about eight hundred and fifty years.

There appeared to be a parallel between the story of Noah's Ark and the 'Ark of the Covenant'. As Noah and his family were safe from harm in the Ark, which the Lord instructed Noah to build, so was the 'Manna' while it was in the 'Ark of the Covenant'. The spiritual application is for those who remain in the presence of the Lord are protected, as our soul and spirit does not rot or decay like our body, but as Paul reminded the Corinthians:

"Therefore we do not lose heart.
Even though our outward man is perishing,
yet the inward man is being renewed day by day."

2 Corinthians 4:16

The Israelites began to celebrate the seven feasts, although the full implications of what each meant were still hidden. Only after they had entered the Promised Land and the wanderings were behind them would the Feast of Tabernacles come with a fuller understanding.

Centralised Worship

About five hundred years had passed from the third Passover, Jericho, with several Judges and many Kings ruling over the children of Israel, to the recorded Passover by Hezekiah. The Passover continued but not in the traditional fashion, as some of the Israelites did not consecrate themselves before the celebration was observed and carried out; however, scripture records Hezekiah centralised worship along with Passover sacrifices and leading the people back to God.

Between the time of Joshua's leadership and Hezekiah's reign, several Judges and Kings ruled over the children of Israel. During this time, the people continued to align with their neighbours, worshipping their foreign pagan gods instead of converting them to the One True God. This was directly against the known will of the Lord, as Israelites were called to be a separate people.

When studying and processing the events after Joshua set up the Tabernacle at Shiloh:

> *"Now the whole congregation of the children of Israel*
> *assembled together at Shiloh,*
> *and set up the Tabernacle of meeting there.*
> *And the land was subdued before them,"*
>
> Joshua 18:1

the Lord had already shared with Moses and Joshua the following:

> *"The Lord said to Moses,*
> *'Behold, you will rest with your fathers;*
> *and this people will rise*
> *and play the harlot with the gods*
> *of the foreigners of the land,*
> *where they go to be among them,*
> *and they will forsake Me and break My covenant*
> *which I have made with them."*
>
> Deuteronomy 31:16

The last verse recorded in the Book of Judges says:

> *"In those days there was no king in Israel;*
> *everyone did what was right in his own eyes."*
>
> Judges 21:25

One could imagine that as 'everyone did what was right in his own eyes', the Covenant which had been given to Moses to be read day and night, the prescribed worship of God only and the Laws given at Mount Sinai, along with the seven feast days, including the sabbaths, were long forgotten, maybe except for a few, a remnant, but we are not told.

The first King of Israel was Saul, as the children of Israel demanded a king and not a judge. Saul was chosen by the Lord, who directed the prophet Samuel to anoint him as the leader of Israel. Although Saul was the anointed king, he thought like the people he ruled and 'did what was right in his own eyes'. Samuel instructed Saul to:

> *"Attack Amalek, and destroy all that they have,*
> *and do not spare them.*
> *But kill both man and woman,*
> *infant and nursing child,*
> *ox and sheep, camel and donkey."*
>
> 1 Samuel 15:3

"But Saul and the people spared Agag, king of the Amalekites, and the best of the sheep, the oxen, the fatlings, the lambs, and all that was good, and were unwilling to utterly destroy them. But everything despised and worthless, they utterly destroyed." 1 Samuel 15:9

Samuel confronts Saul, who is very pleased with himself and boasts to Samuel how he carried out the Lord's instructions. Samuel's reply to Saul left him in no doubt as to his indiscretion and failure to comply with the known will of Father God.

> *"What then is this bleating of the sheep in my ears, and the lowing of the oxen which I hear?"*
>
> 1 Samuel 15:14

Partial obedience is not obedience, as this led Saul to be rejected by the Lord. Samuel was within his right to pass the judgement of the Lord onto Saul as he had chosen to disobey and keep the best for themselves. This was a holy war as all the spoil was considered a sacrifice to the Lord, so when Saul took the best for himself, this action was a direct rebellion against Father God.

However, because Saul sinned in the sight of the Lord, he was replaced with David, the son of Jesse, who Samuel anointed in front of his family. Under the anointing of the Holy Spirit, David fought Goliath and won the battle, which led him to marry the daughter of Saul called Michal (1 Samuel 18:27b). King Saul resented David when he heard the women as they sang and danced said:

> *"Saul has slain his thousands, and David his ten thousands."*
>
> 1 Samuel 18:7

Saul became so bitter, jealous, and angry against David that David fled from Saul. In his pursuit of David, Saul inquired about the whereabouts of David. Doeg the Edomite, who was set over the servants of Saul, told him:

> *"I saw the son of Jesse going to Nob,*
> *to Ahimelech the son of Ahitub.*
> *And he inquired of the Lord for him,*
> *gave him provisions, and gave him*
> *the sword of Goliath the Philistine."*
>
> 1 Samuel 22:9–10

Saul went and confronted Ahimelech, the priest, but Saul became so enraged with hatred for what the priests had done to help David that Saul commanded Doeg to kill all the priests, and he killed eighty-five men who wore a linen ephod. As Nob was the city of priests, Saul had all the inhabitants struck with the edge of the sword, both men and women, children and nursing infants, oxen and donkeys and sheep. 1 Samuel 22:18–19

Eventually, after the death of Saul, David brought unity to Israel as he ruled under the directions of the Lord, for we are told:

> *"David did what was right*
> *in the eyes of the Lord,*
> *and had not turned aside from anything*

> *that He commanded him all the days of his life,*
> *except in the matter of Uriah the Hittite."*
>
> 1 Kings 15:5

Although David was able to bring the Ark of the Covenant to Jerusalem and placed it in the midst of the Tabernacle that David had erected for it (1 Chronicles 16:1), and established regular worship, we are told that:

> *"Zadok the priest and his brethren the priests,*
> *burnt offerings to the Lord on the altar*
> *of burnt offering regularly morning and evening,*
> *and to do according to all that is written*
> *in the Law of the Lord*
> *which He commanded Israel."*
>
> 1 Chronicles 16:39–40

David placed the Ark of the Covenant in the Tabernacle he had made near Jerusalem, which is referred to as the Tabernacle of David. The original Tent of Meeting, the Tabernacle of Moses, and its altar remained in Gibeon.

When David was dying, his wife Bathsheba requested the prophet Nathan to remind David that he had promised the kingship to Solomon (1 Chronicles 22:9–11). Solomon was never trained to be king of Israel, as he was not David's first-born son. This is reflected when Solomon requested help from the Lord to govern the children as his father did (1 Kings 3:7). Solomon was privileged to replace both Tabernacles that his father David had used with a new structure called 'Solomon's Temple'.

While Solomon is remembered for his earthly wisdom, when spiritual wisdom was required, the following verses record his failure to worship the One true God, as did his father, David.

> *"For it was so, when Solomon was old,*
> *that his wives turned his heart after other gods;*
> *and his heart was not loyal to the Lord his God,*
> *as was the heart of his father David."*
> *"Solomon did evil in the sight of the Lord,*
> *and did not fully follow the Lord,*
> *as did his father David."*
>
> 1 Kings 11:4, 6

After the death of Solomon, the kingdom was divided, split into two, the Northern and Southern Kingdoms, or Israel and Judah. The nineteen kings who ruled over Israel were all evil kings and did not do what was right in the sight of the Lord. As history revealed, the Northern Kingdom was eventually overthrown by the Assyrians and led away into captivity. The Southern Kingdom, or Judah, had twenty kings, but the difference was that eight were good kings who followed the ways and instructions of the Lord.

Kings of Israel

Saul
David
Solomon

—DIVIDED KINGDOM—

Kings of Israel

Jeroboam I	Evil	1 Kings 13:33–34; 14:8–9
Nadab	Evil	1 Kings 15:25–26
Baasha	Evil	1 Kings 15:33–34
Elah	Evil	1 Kings 16:12–13
Zimri	Evil	1 Kings 16:18–19
Omri	Evil	1 Kings 16:25
Ahab	Evil	1 Kings 16:30
Ahaziah	Evil	1 Kings 22:51–52
Jehoram	Evil	2 Kings 3:1–2
Jehu	Evil	2 Kings 10:31
Jehoahaz	Evil	2 Kings 13:1–2
Jehoash	Evil	2 Kings 13:10–11
Jeroboam II	Evil	2 Kings 14:23–24
Zechariah	Evil	2 Kings 15:8–9
Shallum	Evil	2 Kings 15:13–15
Menahem	Evil	2 Kings 15:17–18
Pekahiah	Evil	2 Kings 15:23–24
Pekah	Evil	2 Kings 15:27–28
Hoshea	Evil	2 Kings 17:1–2

—ASSYRIAN CAPTIVITY, 2 KINGS 17:6—

Kings of Judah

Rehoboam	Evil	1 Kings 14:21–22
Abijam	Evil	1 Kings 15;1–3
Asa	Good	1 Kings 15:11
Jehoshaphat	Good	2 Chronicles 17:3–4
Jehoram	Evil	2 Kings 8:16–18
Ahaziah	Evil	2 Kings 8:26–27
Athaliah	Evil	2 Kings 11:1–20
Joash (Jehoash)	Good	2 Kings 12:1–2
Amaziah	Good	2 Kings 14:1–3
Azaria (Uzziah)	Good	2 Kings 15:1–3
Jotham	Good	2 Kings 15:32–34
Ahaz	Evil	2 Kings 16:1–2
Hezekiah	Good	2 Kings 18:1–3
Manasseh	Evil	2 Kings 21:1–2
Amon	Evil	2 Kings 21:19–20
Josiah	Good	2 Kings 22:1–2
Jehoahaz	Evil	2 Kings 23:31–32
Jehoiakim	Evil	2 Kings 23:36–37
Jehoiachin	Evil	2 Kings 24:8–9
Zedekiah	Evil	2 Kings 24:18–19

—BABYLONIAN CAPTIVITY—

About two hundred years had passed since the death of Solomon, Hezekiah was 25 years old when he was made king of Judah. Some of his predecessors had desecrated the Temple by allowing the worship of other gods to be carried out. Eventually, the Temple was closed and fell into disrepair, but as Hezekiah was young and enthusiastic, he reopened the Temple, carried out many repairs and removed all that was an abomination to the Lord.

Hezekiah was well aware of the idolatrous worship that the people of Judah were participating in, so he established new regulations that would change the Passover celebrations and impact the Passover worship in the future. The Passover celebration instituted by Hezekiah was different to that celebrated in Egypt under Moses' guidance.

The Exodus Passover was a family celebration, but this changed when Passover worship was centralised by Hezekiah. The priests and Levites started inspecting and sacrificing the Passover lambs at the Temple for the people instead of the head of the household sacrificing them at their home. Many of the people were also ceremonially unclean, so the priests and Levites took their place. 2 Chronicles 30:17

King Hezekiah called for the centralisation of the Passover to be carried out at the Temple in Jerusalem (2 Chronicles 29:20–36; 30:5, v17), which created logistic problems because it was impossible for the priests and Levites to sacrifice so many Passover lambs between sundown and sunset on the fourteenth.

As a result, killing the Passover lambs continued all day through the daytime of the prescribed day.

Hezekiah sent a letter to some of the other tribes, but they laughed and scorned his invitation, although some accepted and came to Jerusalem. After the priests and Levites had purified themselves, the priests sprinkled some of the blood from the lamb they received from the hand of the Levites on the altar. 2 Chronicles 30:16

> *"So there was great joy in Jerusalem,*
> *for since the time of Solomon the son of David,*
> *king of Israel,*
> *there had been nothing like this in Jerusalem."*
>
> 2 Chronicles 30:26

The Passover had taken on somewhat of a formality, away from the family celebration. Rights and privileges that belonged to the head of the house were now given to the priest to check that the lamb offered for sacrifice was without blemish. The lamb would be slain by the Levite, and the blood would be given to the priest, who would sprinkle it on the altar then the head of the family would return to their home, but as the prescribed hour for the killing was anywhere but sundown or twilight, the original Passover prescribed by the Lord was slowly modified to suit a changing generation and those who would follow.

A few years passed when King Josiah reigned over the children of Israel and was one of the few good kings. Hilkiah, the priest, found the 'Book of the Law' and gave the book to Shaphan, the scribe.

> *"Then Shaphan the scribe told the king, saying,*
> *'Hilkiah the priest has given me a book'.*
> *And Shaphan read it before the king."*
>
> 2 Chronicles 34:18

Solomon's Temple was filled with idolatrous worship by many kings, perhaps the 'Book of the Law' written by Moses would have been hidden away out of sight, out of mind. The Laws given to Moses by the Lord, with only the worship of God permitted, would have had an impact on those who instigated the worship of other gods. Specific instructions were given to Joshua as to the reading of the Law, for it is written:

> *"This Book of the Law shall not depart from your mouth,*
> *but you shall meditate in it day and night,*
> *that you may observe to do*
> *according to all that is written in it.*
> *For then you will make your way prosperous,*
> *and then you will have good success."*
>
> Joshua 1:8

The observance of the Law was the core of Israel's future success as a nation, but as they were disobedient in so many ways since the days in Egypt, throughout their whole history, would anything else have taken place than what has been revealed in their history and how they perceived the Law was to be obeyed?

After King Josiah had heard what was written in the 'Book of the Law', he carried out the Passover but encountered the same problems as King Hezekiah concerning logistics (2 Chronicles 35:1–19). As Josiah was one of the good kings, he restored true worship and kept the Passover. Josiah removed all the abominations from the country that belonged to the children of Israel. While the Temple was cleansed and repaired, Josiah gave the following directions to the Levites:

"Put the holy ark in the house
which Solomon the son of David,
king of Israel, built.
It shall no longer be a burden on your shoulders.
Now serve the Lord your God and His people Israel."

2 Chronicles 35:3

This prompts the question as to where was the 'Ark of the Covenant' because this was the first article to be made, where the Lord would manifest Himself to the children of Israel in the Tabernacle?

> *"King Josiah also gave the lay people lambs and young goats from the flock, all for Passover offerings for all who were present, to the number of thirty thousand, as well as three thousand cattle; these were from the king's possessions."* 2 Chronicles 35:7

As King Josiah had commanded the Passover to be carried out according to the 'Book of Moses', the priests stood in their places, and the Levites in their divisions, and slaughtered the Passover offerings. The priests sprinkled the blood with their hands, while the Levites skinned the animals (2 Chronicles 35:10). The children of Israel who were present kept the Passover at that time and the Feast of Unleavened Bread for seven days. No other Passover had been kept in Israel as King Josiah had commanded, since the days of Samuel the prophet. 2 Chronicles 35:18a

After all the kings had served their reigns and the Southern Kingdom of Judah had been taken away by the Babylonians, nearly sixty years passed from the captivity, and some of the exiled children of Israel returned to Jerusalem, along with the Priest Ezra as their leader (Ezra 6:19–22).

> *"King Cyrus also brought out the articles*
> *of the house of the Lord,*
> *which Nebuchadnezzar had taken*
> *from Jerusalem and put in the temple*
> *of his gods."*
>
> Ezra 1:7

What was given to them were the things in the house of the Lord, which included platers, knives, basins and other minor articles (Ezra 1:8–11), but not the main parts within the Tabernacle, as these had been destroyed. 2 Kings 24:13

The returned exiles found Solomon's Temple in disarray, so they set to work and carried out the necessary cleaning, repairs and dedication. As all was in place, Ezra called the people to celebrate the Passover.

On the fourteenth day of the first month, the priests and Levites purified themselves, as they were required to be ritually clean in preparation for the Passover celebration. The Levites slaughtered the Passover lambs for the descendants of the captivity, themselves and the priests.

> *"Then the children of Israel*
> *who had returned from the captivity*
> *ate together with all who had separated themselves*
> *from the filth of the nations of the land*
> *in order to seek the Lord God of Israel."*
>
> Ezra 6:21

This was a joyful occasion for the returned exiles who had separated themselves for the Lord. They also shared in the Feast of Unleavened Bread, which was part of the Passover Feasts for the seven prescribed days. Their joyful attitude had a profound impact on the king of Assyria as he encouraged and strengthened their hands in the work of the house of God, the God of Israel. One could imagine that these people were the remnant of those who had survived through the nineteen evil kings of Israel.

About nine hundred and fifty years had passed since the Passover in Egypt to the joyous celebration of the Passover by the exiled Israelites when they returned from Babylon to Jerusalem. What had been commanded to observe was a family meal of whole roast lamb, separated for four days, killed at twilight, eaten with bitter herbs and unleavened bread, which had been modified to suit the times and situations of the people.

While the Passover regulations had been set down by the Lord as a yearly celebration, along with the other joyful six feasts, much had been destroyed or neglected with what the Lord had put in place. While the lamb and the unleavened bread remained constant, the bitter herbs could have been fraught with their own hardships over the many years.

The Tabernacle was a thing of the past, and the Temple Solomon built was desecrated time and time again, with heathen gods substituted for the One True God of Israel. How many times was it shut up, then reopened, refurbished and then shut down again? So many evil leaders, yet so few good ones who would lead the people in their righteous way of thinking and worship. What the future held for the chosen people of the Lord would be revealed as the remnant sought the truth.

First Temple Timeline

Date	Comment
960 BC	King Solomon dedicates his Temple.
931 BC	Solomon dies and his kingdom is divided: Northern Kingdom (Israel) and Southern Kingdom (Judah).
901 BC	Temple treasures taken by Egyptian Pharaoh Shishak (1 Kings 14:25–28; 2 Chron. 12:1–11).
835 BC	Jehoash, King of Judah and Jehoiada repair damaged parts of the Temple (2 Kings 12:5–14; 2 Chron. 24:12–14).
826 BC	Joash, King of Israel attacks Judah, breaks down the walls of Jerusalem, plunders the temple taking the Temple treasury to Samaria (2 Kings 14:13–14).
742–735 BC	King Jothan, son of Uzziah, builds the upper gate of the Temple (2 Kings 15:35; 2 Chron. 27:3).
722 BC	Northern Kingdom falls to Assyria.
720 BC	King Ahaz closes the Temple, empties the temple treasury, breaks up the Temple furnishings to pay tribute to Assyrian king, Tiglath–Pileser III, and defiles the Temple with a pagan Syrian altar (2 Kings 16:8–18; 2 Chron. 28:21, 24).
715 BC	King Hezekiah opens the Temple doors, cleanses the Temple, returns temple vessels, restores ritual and Passover (2 Chron. 29:3–19; 30:1–27; 31:11–12).
711 BC	Hezekiah is forced to give up the Temple treasuries and strip gold off the Temple doors to pay tribute to the Assyrian king Sennacherib (2 Kings 18:15–16).
700 BC	Hezekiah foolishly shows the temple treasures to the prince of Babylon, who eventually plunded the Temple (2 Kings 20:12–21; 2 Chron. 32:31).
695–642 BC	King Manasseh of Judah places idols in the Temple including the Holy Place and the Holy of Holies. The Ark was removed by faithful Levites to prevent their defilement (2 Kings 21:4–7; 2 Chron. 33:7–9, 15).
622 BC	King Joshiah of Judah restored the Temple (2 Kings 22:8; 2 Chron. 35:3). He commands the Levites to return the Ark (2 Chron. 35:3).

Centralised Worship

Date	Comment
605 BC	Babylon King Nebuchadnezzar ransacks the Temple, taking articles and depositing them in the Babylon temple at Shinar (2 Chron. 36:7).
597 BC	Nebuchadnezzar returns and further plunders the treasures of the Temple (2 Kings 24:13; 2 Chron. 36:7).
586 BC	Nebuchadnezzar invades Jerusalem a third time, destroys the Temple. Southern Kingdom of Judah falls to Babylon and Jews taken captive.

Jesus, The Passover Lamb

"Now the feast of Unleavened Bread drew near,
which is called Passover."
"The disciples came to Jesus,
aying to Him,
'Where do You want us to prepare
for You to eat the Passover?'."

Luke 22:1, Matthew 26:17b

About fourteen hundred years passed since the second Passover in the Sinai desert, about seven hundred years from the time of Hezekiah to Jesus sharing His last Passover meal with His disciples. Solomon's Temple had been plundered on a few occasions, and the faithful had completed refurbishing and restoration. Herod, a Roman governor, began rebuilding Solomon's Temple in about 20 BC and renamed the new structure Herod's Temple. By the time Jesus and His disciples were in Jerusalem, Herod's Temple was a sight to behold.

The question could be asked, "Had the Passover Ceremony changed since Hezekiah's time?" A second question could be,

"Who was Jesus, and why did His coming change the Passover observance?" A little history into the ancestry of two blessed families should help clarify the importance of what God had ordained to take place.

The Bible does not contain the names of all those who were used by Father God to bring about His desired will. An unnamed husband and wife, a blessed family had two daughters. One was Elizabeth, who married Zachariah and was chosen to have John the Baptist in their old age, whereas Elizabeth's sister, the other daughter, married Heli, who had two daughters.

One of the two daughters, born to Heli and his wife, was Mary, who eventually married Joseph and was chosen to have the Messiah, Jesus Christ. The other daughter, Salome, the

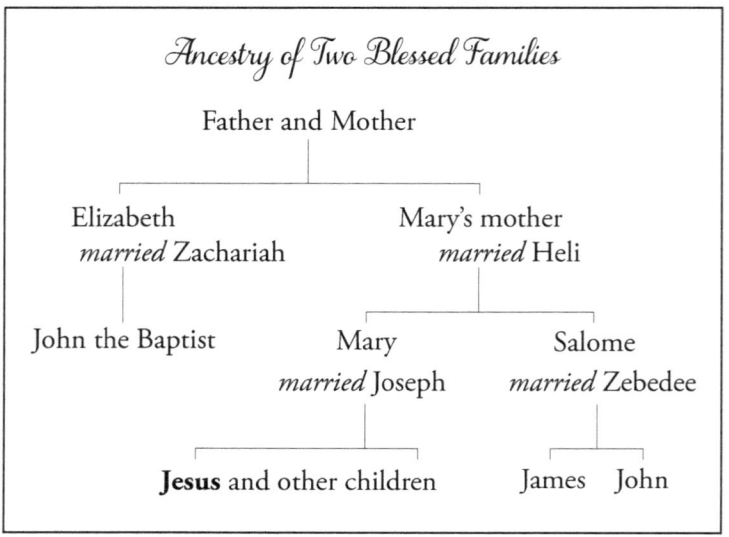

younger sister of Mary, married Zebedee and was chosen to have James and John. Elizabeth was chosen to have John the Baptist, the forerunner to Jesus; her niece, Mary, would bear Jesus the Messiah and the younger sister, Salome, would bear two sons, James and John, who would take the Message of Jesus and what He accomplished to the world.

Jesus was about seven years old when He returned from Egypt to Nazareth with His parents, Joseph and Mary. The following scripture is recorded:

> *"His parents went to Jerusalem*
> *every year at the Feast of Passover.*
> *And when He was twelve years old,*
> *they went to Jerusalem*
> *according to the custom of the feast."*
>
> Luke 2:42–42

A further reading adds more information about Jesus:

> *"When they (Jesus family) had finished the days,*
> *as they returned,*
> *the Boy Jesus lingered behind in Jerusalem.*
> *And Joseph and His mother did not know it."*

> *"All who heard Him were astonished*
> *at His understanding and answers."*
>
> Luke 2:43, v47

Joseph and Mary had travelled for three days with the other members of their family when they realised Jesus was missing, so they returned to Jerusalem to find Him. When they found Jesus sitting in the temple among the teachers, both listening to them and asking questions, Mary approached Him and said:

> *"Son, why have You done this to us?*
> *Look, Your father and I have sought You anxiously."*
> *And He said to them,*
> *"Why did you seek Me?*
> *Did you not know that I must be*
> *about My Father's business?"*
>
> Luke 2:48b–49

"Then He went down with them and came to Nazareth, and was subject to them, but His mother kept all these things in her heart." Luke 2:51

About seventeen years would pass before both John and Jesus would be called by Father God to follow the path He had mapped out for them and their calling. John was the forerunner to Jesus, as he fulfilled the prophecy of Isaiah when he said:

> *"Prepare the way of the Lord;*
> *make straight in the desert*
> *a highway for our God."*
>
> *"The glory of the Lord shall be revealed,*
> *and all flesh shall see it together;*
> *for the mouth of the Lord has spoken."*
>
> Isaiah 40:3b, v5

John the Baptist, the second cousin of Jesus, was preaching 'Repentance' near the Jordan River and the remission of sins to any who would be baptised. He preached about One who would come after Him whose sandals He was not worthy to unlatch. John 1:27

On one particular day, John was preaching and baptising when he saw Jesus walking toward him. As He came near him, John cried out, *"Behold the Lamb of God, who takes away the sin of the world."* (John 1:29b) Andrew, Peter's brother and John, Jesus' cousin, both witnessed what had transpired as Jesus approached John the Baptist to be baptised.

John the Baptist was reluctant to baptise Jesus, but after Jesus gave him permission why this was required to be carried out, John baptised Jesus. After Jesus was baptised, which was witnessed by Father God and the Holy Spirit, Jesus left and continued on and into His ministry.

Jesus followed in the steps of His earthly father Joseph as each year He would attend the Passover in Jerusalem, but how Jesus celebrated the Passover is not recorded. One could imagine that what they shared was family time together with relatives in Jerusalem. Once Jesus commenced His three-year ministry, worship at Jerusalem took on a different theme, as He was the Son of God, a different focus became His goal.

Jesus attended four Passovers in His just over three-year ministry. At the beginning of the first year at Passover, He cleansed the Temple and exposed the wrong and the exploitation of many, as He returned the Temple to a place of prayer, not a den of thieves. At His second Passover, Jesus healed a man on the Sabbath, which the authorities saw as blasphemy and wanted to kill Jesus.

At the time of the third Passover, Jesus was ministering in the area around Capernaum in Galilee, in His year of opposition, so he did not travel to Jerusalem for the feast but would have observed the must-attend-feast in the Capernaum area. Jesus fed the five thousand just before the third Passover feast, and the crowds wanted to make Him King, but as John wrote:

> *"After these things Jesus walked in Galilee;*
> *for He did not want to walk in Judea,*
> *because the Jews sought to kill Him."*
>
> John 7:1

Jesus knew He was protected by Father God, as Satan had reminded Jesus:

> *"For He shall give His angels charge over You,*
> *to keep you in all your ways.*
> *In their hands they shall bear you up,*
> *Lest you dash your foot against a stone."*
>
> Psalm 91:11–12

But Jesus quoted the scripture to Satan when He replied:

> *"You shall not tempt the Lord your God."*
>
> Deuteronomy 6:16

Jesus knew that going to Jerusalem would be a deliberate act, as He would be tempting His Father, which would break the Law and cause Him to sin. About six months had passed as the Feast of Tabernacles, the third -must-attend feast, was about to occur. The earthly brothers of Jesus encouraged Him to attend the feast and reveal Himself, but Jesus replied:

> *"You go up to the feast.*
> *I am not yet going up to the feast,*
> *for My time has not yet fully come."*
>
> John 7:8

Jesus did attend the Feast of Tabernacles, and just as He had expected, the Jewish leaders sought to kill Him, but as the authorities were afraid of the crowd and their reaction to them, they withdrew and sought another time to kill Jesus.

Before the fourth Passover, Jesus made His way to Jerusalem as He knew this would be His last earthly Passover. Part of the Passover preparations was that those who would take part were to be purified seven days before the feast. As Jesus was the spotless, sinless Son of God, He had no reason to carry out this law. This is explained in the words of Jesus when He said:

"Do not think that I came
to destroy the Law or the Prophets.
I did not come to destroy but to fulfil.
For assuredly, I say to you,
till heaven and earth pass away,
one jot or tittle will by no means pass
from the law till all is fulfilled."

Matthew 5:17–18

Seven days before Passover, Jesus and His disciples were staying at Bethany in the home of Martha, Lazarus and Mary, as Jesus and His disciples would travel every day from Bethany to Jerusalem and return. Four days before the Passover, Jesus would have arranged for the lamb to be separated and kept at the place where He and His disciples would share the Passover.

The disciples were not privy to the location, but on the same day, Judas contracted with the priests to betray Jesus and deliver Him to them. Judas had successfully separated the Lamb of God from the world. Luke 22:4

When it was time for Jesus and the disciples to celebrate the Passover, according to the Gospel of Luke, Jesus sent Peter and John to Jerusalem to prepare the meal for them all to commemorate. The time when the lamb was to be killed was crucial at the appointed time was to be celebrated, not what the authorities were doing. The prescribed time is set out in the following way.

"On the fourteenth day of this month,

at twilight,

you shall keep the Passover

at its appointed time."

Numbers 9:3

Twilight is explained as the period of time after sunset and before sunrise, or as it is referred to in the Jewish culture, between the evenings. Because the killing of the Passover lamb was now centralised, the time extended way past the time set for the sacrifice in the first Passover and was a logistical disaster for the priests. As Jewish days went from sunset to sunset or 6 pm to 6 pm, the killing of the lambs extended into the next day, and the Passover feast was eaten on the second day, the 'Feast of Unleavened Bread'.

Jesus observed the original Passover as He possibly, at 6:05 pm on the 14th of Nissan, the Passover lamb would be slaughtered, skinned, guttered and roasted. Around 9 pm, Jesus and His disciples would be enjoying the Passover celebrations, as Jesus said:

> *"With fervent desire I have desired*
> *to eat this Passover with you before I suffer,*
> *for I say to you, I will no longer eat of it*
> *until it is fulfilled in the kingdom of God."*
>
> Luke 22:15–16

Before the Passover meal is considered, let us follow the day of Jesus as hour by hour passed. Jesus was arrested in Gethsemane, questioned by Annas, then Caiaphas, the high priest. The Sanhedrin found Jesus guilty of blasphemy but never considered He was telling the truth. Jesus was questioned by Pilate, then Herod, and back to Pilate, who handed him over to the soldiers for crucifixion. By 9 am, Jesus was nailed to the cross and at 3 pm, He committed Himself to the Father, as He yielded up His Spirit.

When Jesus reclined with His disciples at the Passover table, the roasted lamb, unleavened bread and bitter herbs would all be present as they recalled the Passover of the Hebrews so many years previous. This was a family meal as Jesus referred to His followers as His mother and brothers, for He said:

> *"For whoever does the will*
> *of My Father in heaven is*
> *My brother and sister and mother."*

Matthew 12:50

After the Passover story was recalled and shared, Jesus did something out of the ordinary. In front of all the disciples, Jesus spoke the following words:

> *"Assuredly, I say to you,*
> *one of you will betray Me.*
> *He who dipped his hand with Me in the dish*
> *will betray Me."*
> *Then Judas said, "Rabbi, is it I?"*
> *Jesus said to him, "You have said it."*

Matthew 26:21, v23, v25

The question required to be asked is, "What was the dish?" It wasn't a cup of wine as the verse said *'dish'*. An archaeology study and recent research suggested that a bean stew, lamb, olives, bitter herbs, a fish sauce, unleavened bread, dates, and wine could be part of the menu at the Passover. Fish sauce could be the obvious choice, as Jesus referred to Peter as a 'fisher of men' (Luke 5:10), but something else from the past could be contained within the food on the table.

Trials of Jesus and Outcome

Sequence	Investigation and Penalty	Outcome	Notes	Time *(approx)*
Arrest in the Garden of Gethsemane.	Seeking Jesus.	Arrested. Led away bound to Annas.		1 am
1. Trial by Annas.	Examined.	Sent to son-in-law Caiaphas.	Annas was the previous high priest.	2 am
2. Trial by Caiaphas.	Questioned and interrogated.	Caiaphas enraged. Tore his clothes. Sent Jesus to Sanhedrin.	By tearing his clothes, Caiaphas became ritually unclean and therefore ceased from any further involvement with Jesus. Annas took his place. Leviticus 21:10 is the law governing this act.	2:30 am
3. Trial by Sanhedrin.	Blasphemy.	Found guilty.	This was the first legal trial held in daylight.	4:30 am
4. Trial by Pilate	Questioned.	Pilate recognises that Jesus is a Galilean and therefore sent Him to Herod who is in charge of Galilee.		6 am
5. Trial by Herod.	Questioned.	Made sport of Jesus. Put on Him a purple robe. Sent Jesus back to Pilate.		6:30 am

Jesus, the Passover Lamb

Sequence	Investigation and Penalty	Outcome	Notes	Time *(approx)*
6. Trial by Pilate.	Questioned and interrogated.	Found Innocent. Because Pilate feared offending Caesar, he gave Jesus over to the Jews to crucify.	Pilate was aware the Jewish leaders were jealous of Jesus and His ministry. Because Jesus had answered Pilate that He was a King, this was treason against Caesar and Rome.	7:00 am
Given to soldiers.	They made sport of Jesus and scourged Him.	Bleeding, bruised. A crown of thorns on His head.	Jesus was redressed. The purple seamless robe given to Him by Herod adorned Him.	8:00am
Taken to be crucified.	Nailed on the Cross at 9 am	Jesus died after committing His spirit to Father God. The veil in the temple torn in two.	There was no high priest. When Jesus died, the veil ripped from top to bottom. Jesus paid the price. He is now the Great High Priest.	3 pm

"Esau said, "Please feed me some of your red stew,

for I am weary."

"Jacob said, "Sell me your birthright as of this day."

And Esau said, "What is this birthright to me?"

So he swore to Jacob and sold him his birthright."

Genesis 25:31

The red stew that Jacob had cooked was a lentil or bean soup. Remember, Jacob was a farmer, and Esau a hunter. Jesus knew Satan wanted to possess Judas, and through the sop, He offered Judas a way out. Jesus quietly and unobtrusively mentioned what was in the heart of one of the disciples. He did it through an act of love, by dipping His bread into the dish, using the same dish as the man who would sell Him into death.

The act of giving Judas the bread that He dipped in the dish was an act of Jesus' great love for Judas. He had extended His love to Judas as Jesus reached out to him with the deepest kind of love. Although Jesus knew the will of Father God was to be fulfilled through Judas, He could have hoped that Judas would have realised His great love for him through the sop, that even though Judas had planned and turned Him into the enemy, Jesus still considered him as one of His closest friends, as proven by the sop. At this point, Judas could have still repented.

Was Judas saying to Jesus he was weary of following Him as he believed Him to be the Messiah who would lead them out of oppression? That he had followed Him for the last eighteen months, and now he was going to force His hand and make Him reveal the real purpose, as Judas thought, take place? What was the use of following if He did not reveal Himself and take control, so sold his right to the kingdom of God?

But there was something else on the table that had not been mentioned in any of the other Passover meals. On the table were four cups of wine. The four cups represented the four expressions of deliverance promised by the Lord to the children of Israel.

> *"Say to the children of Israel:*
> *I am the Lord; I will bring you out*
> *from under the burdens of the Egyptians,*
> *I will rescue you from their bondage,*
> *and I will redeem you with an outstretched arm*
> *and with great judgements.*
> *I will take you as My people,*
> *and I will be your God."*
>
> Exodus 6:6–7a

1. I will bring them out: The Cup of Sanctification.
2. I will deliver them: The Cup of Deliverance.
3. I will redeem them: The Cup of Redemption.
4. I will take them: The Cup of Praise or Promise.

Jesus referred to the Old Covenant outlined to Moses as they ate together and reminded each of their ancestral heritage and the promises given to them. But then Jesus did something that was not part of the Passover celebration. As the meal was completed, Jesus took some of the unleavened bread, broke it, and shared the bread with each of the eleven disciples who were in His presence.

Not one of the disciples asked Jesus what He was teaching them, as on many occasions, they had no understanding. What Jesus was about to share with them was teaching He had previously taught but had received a mixed response from many of His followers who left. Jesus taught:

"Most assuredly, I say to you, unless you eat the flesh of the Son of Man and drink His blood, you have no life in you. Whoever eats My flesh and drinks My blood has eternal life, and I will raise him up at the last day. For My flesh is food indeed, and My blood is drink indeed. He who eats My flesh and drinks My blood abides in Me, as I in him. As the living Father sent Me, and I live because of the Father, so he who feeds on Me will live because of Me. This is the bread which came down from heaven, not as your fathers ate manna, and are dead. He who eats this bread will live forever."
John 6:53–58

> *"When He had given thanks,*
> *He broke the bread and said,*
> *'Take, eat;*
> *this is My body which is broken for you;*
> *do this in remembrance of Me."*
>
> 1 Corinthians 11:24

As they watched, Jesus picked up the third cup of wine from the table, the 'Cup of Redemption' and said:

> *"This cup is the New Covenant in My blood.*
> *This do,*

as often as you drink it,
in remembrance of Me."

1 Corinthians 11:25

Jesus did not drink from the fourth cup, the 'Cup of Praise', but continued His teaching and sharing with His disciples, for He said:

"Assuredly, I say to you,
I will no longer drink of the fruit of the vine
until that day when I drink it new
in the kingdom of God."

Mark 14:25

Although the disciples did not understand what Jesus had just said, He had replaced the Old Covenant with the New Covenant, which He would bring about by His obedience to the known will of His Father, God.

The Passover meal and Lord's Supper were completed as the disciples sang a hymn before they left. Singing was a joyful part of the celebrations, as the psalms were sung to add a joyous note to the proceedings. Matthew 26:30

The Passover celebrations were completed for Jesus and His disciples, but for the rest of the community, the slaying of the lambs and celebrations were still future, a few hours away. By the time Jesus was nailed to the cross, the priests would be carrying out their priestly duties of slaughtering the lambs, sprinkling the altar with blood, as the Levites skinned the animal and returned the carcass to the owner for roasting later in the day. While they were killing the lambs on the fourteenth, the roasting would be carried out and eaten on the fifteenth, which contravened the Law of Moses.

Chaos came to the busy priests when, at noon, darkness descended, and everything was put on hold. Nothing more could be completed, as they just had to wait. They had no idea what they had unleashed against themselves, but more was to follow. The high priest would normally say at 3 pm, after the last lamb had been slaughtered, "It is finished," but this year was different. At 3 pm, Jesus, knowing all things had been accomplished, said:

"It is finished."

John 19:30

After Jesus had yielded His life into the care of His Father, the earth quaked, the darkness became light, and the temple curtain ripped from top to bottom. He had made the way open again into the presence of Almighty God. Through His suffering and death, the New Covenant had been established. Jesus not only kept the Passover as His Father had commanded but was also the *'Sacrificial Lamb'*, crucified on Passover as the Jews celebrated their time of remembrance of things past.

But there is something else that happened in the temple by a priest three times a day at 9 am, noon, and 3 pm, which is the *'Standing Prayer'*. The prayer contained the words for Understanding, Repentance, Forgiveness, Deliverance from Affliction, Healing, the Righteous Reign of God, and much more.

At 9 am, when Jesus was nailed to the cross, these words were prayed. At noon, when darkness descended, these words were prayed. At 3 pm, when the curtain ripped from top to bottom, I wondered what the priest prayed?

As Jesus observed the Passover as instituted by His Father, He fulfilled the Law, but in doing so, the Passover and the Lord's Supper changed the meaning for the world with the fulfilment of the promises given so many years previous.

> *"I will bless you and make your name great;*
> *and you shall be a blessing.*
> *I will bless those who bless you,*
> *and I will curse him who curses you;*
> *and in you all the families of the earth*
> *shall be blessed."*

Genesis 12:2b–3

Jesus had fulfilled what was necessary to institute the New Covenant. While Moses was used by God to lead and teach the children of Israel, Jesus, the Son of God, had, through His suffering and death, made an atonement for the whole world, that whosoever will may be saved. Jesus opened the way for the Comforter, the Holy Spirit, to indwell man's soul where before, the Law restricted mankind's communion and ability to understand and be one with the Father.

The Jewish leaders and race had arrived at a spiritual fork in the road. They could continue the road they had travelled for hundreds of years, or they could take a different road and follow the leading of the Holy Spirit. When Caiaphas asked Jesus if He was the Son of God, Jesus answered truthfully to the question with the words, "Yes I am." The Sanhedrin and the priests had reached a fork in the road. There were two roads they could walk. One led to the Promised Land, and the other led to death, destruction and eternal wanderings.

As the verdict of blasphemy was reached, they, as a nation, had chosen to travel down the path that led to eternal damnation. The left road was physical, whereas the right road was spiritual, but they had no idea what was in store for them, as they were blinded by their own desires and worldly acclaim chose the praise of men rather than the way of Father God.

As they followed their own desires, forty years of warnings were given to them in ways that should have been obvious, but they had made and executed the wrong decision. As the Temple curtain was ripped from top to bottom, as the power of the Holy Spirit was released, lives were changed and the news of salvation spread without the sacrificial system in place.

Jesus, the Passover Lamb

Old Covenant Law	Scripture	New Covenant Grace	Scripture
Old Covenant came by Moses	John 1:17a	New Covenant came by Jesus Christ	John 1:17b
Old Covenant led to death	Proverbs 14:12	New Covenant gives life	2 Corinthians 3:6
Old Covenant cannot give life	2 Corinthians 3:7	New Covenant gives life	Galatians 3:11, 6:8
Old Covenant brought a curse	Galatians 3:10	New Covenant redeemed from the curse	Galatians 3:13
Old Covenant exposed sin	Galatians 3:19	New Covenant covers sin	Romans 4:1–8
Old Covenant enslaved to sin	Galatians 5:1	New Covenant brought freedom from sin	John 8:32, v36
Old Covenant is by works	Hebrews 8:7	New Covenant is living by faith	Galatians 3:10–11
Old Covenant is a shadow	Colosians 2:14–17	New Covenant is the reality	Hebrews 10:1–18
Old Covenant had an earthly priest	Hebrews 5:1–4	New Covenant has a heavenly priest	Hebrews 9:24, 10:12
Old Covenant had many high priests	Hebrews 7:23	New Covenant has only one high priest, Jesus Christ	Hebrews 7:24–28
Old Covenant priesthood was in the lineage of Aaron	Exodus 28:1–43	New Covenant priesthood is in the Melchisedec lineage	Hebrews 7:11–12
Old Covenant priests were sinners	Hebrews 5:1–4	New Covenant, the priest has no sin, Jesus Christ	Hebrews 7:26
Old Covenant had an earthly Tabernacle	Hebrews 9:2	New Covenant has a heavenly tabernacle	Hebrews 8:2
Old Covenant is for Israelites only	Deuteronomy 4:7–8	New Covenant is for all men, the whosoever	Luke 22:20
Old Covenant needed statutes and ordinances	2 Kings 17:37–39	New Covenant only needs your heart	Matthew 22:37
Old Covenant law was written on stone tablets	Exodus 31:18, 32:16	New Covenant is written in people's hearts	Jeremiah 31:33
Old Covenant leaves man imperfect	Hebrews 8:7–8	New Covenant made man perfect in Jesus	Hebrews 7:19
Old Covenant demanded works	Romans 2:13	New Covenant demands obedience	Ephesians 2:8–10
Old Covenant remembered sin	Hebrews 10:3	New Covenant remembered sin no more	Hebrews 8:12, 10:17
Old Covenant ended by Jesus	Romans 10:4	New Covenant established by Jesus	Hebrews 8:6

Destruction of the temple, the massacre of Jerusalem and the Jewish people occurred in AD 70. Their sacrificial system and temple worship were destroyed, never to be restored or rebuilt despite the plans of man. The road to the right passed through Jesus, where spiritual guidance and protection were given through the Holy Spirit. The birth of the church and many who also found salvation through the shed blood of Jesus enabled *'the Called'* to persevere persecution, even to the place of death for some who were martyred in the name of Jesus.

While the left road led to heartache and death, the right road would lead eventually to the Promised Land and the New Jerusalem. Decisions made always have a consequence, whether good or bad. The rulers, when dealing with and deciding to crucify Jesus, had no idea of the impact their selfish thoughts, attitudes and decisions would have on their nation in the future.

One of the early kings of Israel wrote in his book the following words:

> *"There is a way*
> *that seems right unto a man,*
> *but in the end,*
> *it is the way of death."*

Proverbs 14:12

The two roads ran parallel for about forty years, and then, in the fullness of time, the parting of the way was revealed. The left road came to a dead end, or rough dirt road filled with potholes and fraught with danger, while the right road eventually turned to gold, although the early part was dangerous, filled with obstacles and wild spiritual creatures that would devour anyone who thought to travel this road.

Our Companion, along with His rod and staff, comforted all those as they passed through a valley so filled with death, but for those who travelled, they found what they thought was dangerous was just shadows. Psalm 23:1–6

Where the Old Covenant promised an earthly land in Canaan, the New Covenant made the way open for a New Heaven and a New Earth. Under the Old Covenant, people were slaves to sin, but through the sacrificial offering of Jesus, we are set free from sin. Where the Lord chose a people of one nation, we are invited from every nation. While some were called in the Old Covenant to be priests, in the New Covenant, we are *'the Called'*, a Royal Priesthood, a holy nation. Mount Sinai was replaced with Mount Zion, the City of God. We are to worship God only in obedience to Him. Where God's presence was seen in the Tabernacle, we have His presence with us always through the indwelling presence of the Holy Spirit.

	The Old Covenant	**The New Covenant**
God promised His people		
a land in	Canaan	New Jerusalem. New Heaven. New Earth
God rescued His people		
from	Slavery in Egypt	Slavery to sin
by	Moses, who was sent by God to rescue them	Jesus, sent by God
God chose for Himself a special people		
from	The Nation of Israel	Every Nation
whose job was	To be priests	A royal priesthood, a holy nation
God made a covenant with His people		
at	Mt Sinai	Mt Zion
through	Moses	Jesus
that they would	Obey Him and worship Him only	Obey Him and worship Him only
God chose to live with His people	In the Tabernacle	Through His Spirit

The Passover Replaced

Moses to Jesus

Moses built and used the Tabernacle to carry out the Passover celebration, but David wanted to build a Temple. The Lord told David that Solomon would build the Temple in Jerusalem about 1000 BC, with the instructions David had given him. The Temple went through restorations under several good kings of Judea, as the evil kings had let the Temple go into disrepair or closed the doors as other pagan worship was in place.

Solomon's Temple was destroyed in 586 BC when Nebuchadnezzar invaded, conquered the land of Judah, plundered the Temple, and removed everything. The Temple ruins remained dormant until 538 BC, when Cyrus, King of Persia, allowed the exiled Jews to return. By 515 BC, the Jewish residents had completed the Temple reconstruction, but in a modest fashion.

The Temple was generally respected for many years until Antiochus IV Epiphanes plundered the Temple in 169 BC and desecrated the Temple in 167 BC as the god Zeus was worshipped.

Judas Maccabeus cleansed and rededicated the Temple and is remembered in the celebration of *'Hanukkah'* or the *'Festival of Lights'*. For more information about his accomplishments, read the *'Second Book of Maccabees'* found in the Apocrypha.

Under Roman occupation, Herod the Great constructed many grand buildings, including a rebuilt temple, but on a grander scale. In 20BC, King Herod enlarged the Temple Mount and rebuilt the temple with the consent of the people, which took forty-six years, and renamed Solomon's Temple Herod's Temple.

Jesus' Last Passover

The day was Tuesday as Jesus left the Temple on His way to Bethany, where Jesus and His disciples would stay the night. As they walked, the disciples came up to Jesus and pointed out to Him the magnificent structure of Herod's Temple. Jesus replied to them:

> *"Do you not see all these things?*
> *Assuredly, I say to you,*
> *not one stone shall be left upon another,*
> *that shall not be thrown down."*

Matthew 24:2

Within a few days, Jesus would be celebrating the 'Passover' with His disciples at a secret location. Jesus had organised for the lamb to be separated four days before it was to be killed and prepared for their 'Passover' feast. They would remember their ancestors, the Hebrews and the Lord passing over them because they were protected by the shed blood of the lamb on the doorposts.

The Passover celebration was about to change. John the Baptist proclaimed that Jesus was the Lamb of God when he baptised Jesus in the Jordan, as Jesus would take away the sins of the world. Although John had been martyred some time previously and never saw his prophecy fulfilled about Jesus, within a few days, the fulfilment would come to pass.

John the Baptist, in his ministry, was teaching remission for sin without the sacrificial system but through true remorse for past sins and water baptism. This was totally against the teaching of the Pharisees, who were so much involved with animal sacrifice as a money-making business while the pretence of doing the revealed work of Father God and the law was carried out.

The Passover Continues

The rulers came from Jerusalem to ask John if he was the coming Messiah and to check on his teaching and methods, but as they were given a negative response and John was not seen as a threat to their business, they left. If only understanding was theirs, they would have known that as a forerunner to Jesus, this was the way repentance would be found in the future, through the shed blood of Jesus, and not in the sacrificial efforts they were using.

After the death, resurrection, and ascension of Jesus and the Holy Spirit was imparted to the disciples, many Gentiles, along with Jews, embraced the new form of worship, as it superseded what had happened in the past with satisfaction and fulfilment not found in sacrificial worship. Sacrificial worship was no longer required because Jesus was the ultimate sacrificial Lamb sent by Father God. Many Gentiles and Jews left Jerusalem to discover a new life with others who also embraced this new way of living a Spirit-filled life.

When Caiaphas asked Jesus if He was the Son of God, Jesus answered truthfully to the question with the words, "Yes I am." The Sanhedrin and the priests had reached a fork in the road. There were two roads they could walk. One led to the Promised Land, and the other led to death, destruction and eternal wanderings. As the verdict of blasphemy was reached, they, as a nation, had chosen to travel down the path that led to eternal damnation.

The left road was physical, whereas the right road was spiritual, but they had no idea what was in store for them. They were blinded by their desires and worldly acclaim, as they chose the praise of men rather than the way of Father God. The road to the right passed through Jesus, where spiritual guidance and protection were given through the Holy Spirit.

The birth of the church and many who also found salvation through the shed blood of Jesus enabled *'the Called'* to persevere persecution, even to the place of death for some who were martyred in the name of Jesus. While the left road led to heartache and death, the right road would lead eventually to the promised land and the New Jerusalem.

Decisions made always have a consequence, whether good or bad. The rulers, when dealing with and deciding to crucify Jesus, had no idea of the impact their selfish thoughts, attitudes and decisions would have on their nation in the future. One of the early kings of Israel wrote in his book the following words:

> *"There is a way*
> *that seems right unto a man,*
> *but in the end,*
> *it is the way of death."*
>
> Proverbs 14:12

The two roads ran parallel for about forty years, and then, in the fullness of time, the parting of the way was known. The left road came to a dead end, or rough dirt road filled with potholes and fraught with danger.

An eloquent preacher named Apollos, who was mighty in scripture, came through Ephesus (Acts 18:24), but he only knew the baptism of John. This meant Apollos knew that Christ the Messiah had come and fulfilled John's prophecies, but he didn't know the significance of Christ's death and resurrection, the ministry of the indwelling Holy Spirit, or the mystery of the church containing both Jews and Gentiles.

Apollos was a Jewish teacher from Alexandria who preached the baptism of repentance that John the Baptist taught (Mark 1:2–8). He had submitted to John's baptism while it was still valid. He may have been one of John's disciples. According to Paul's statement in Acts 19:4, men were to submit to John's baptism and then believe in Jesus, who would come after. Apollos believed in Jesus after receiving a valid baptism and then being taught the way of God more perfectly (v 26).

Paul had departed from Athens and went to Corinth, where he found a Jew named Aquila, born in Pontus, who had recently moved from Italy with his wife Priscilla to Rome. Claudius had commanded all the Jews to depart from Rome, so they left and went to Corinth, where they met Paul. As they were all tent makers, common ground was found, so they all stayed together for some time until the three moved to Ephesus, where Paul left them and continued his journey to Antioch.

Priscilla and her husband Aquila listened to Apollos preach and realised although he knew his subject well, he had not been baptised by the Holy Spirit, so they took Apollos aside and explained these things to him (Acts 18:24–26). Both Aquila and Priscilla possessed an in-depth understanding of doctrine learned from Paul, and this husband and wife team was able to pass it on to another Christian and build him up in the faith. Acts 18:26–28

Apollos ministered in Corinth after Paul had established the church there (1 Corinthians 3:5–6). Although there was some division in the Corinthian church as to teaching, Paul made the point straight: it was not about who preaches and teaches but about the Lord who brought the increase. Paul wrote:

> *"I planted, Apollos watered,*
> *but God gave the increase.*
> *So then neither he who plants is anything,*
> *nor he who waters,*
> *but God who gives the increase."*
>
> 1 Corinthians 3:6–7

Paul, when writing to Titus in AD 65, acknowledged that Apollos was still preaching the word and maintaining the faith diligently as the Holy Spirit gave him a commission to preach the gospel (Titus 3:13). Aquila and Priscilla continued to use their homes as a church, as Paul referred to them when writing his second letter to Timothy (2 Timothy 4:19) in AD 67. Only a short time passed when Paul, during his final imprisonment in Rome under the rule of Nero, was martyred.

Most of the disciples had faced martyrdom of some kind. James Zebedee in about the year 44 AD, James the Just about 62 AD, Peter crucified upside down about the same time as Paul was martyred. Only the disciple John lived to hear about the destruction of Herod's Temple as he died of old age sometime around 100 AD after he was imprisoned on the Isle of Patmos, but was released to relive in Ephesus.

The Timeline of Paul's Ministry

Date	Event	Reference	Comments
AD 35	Paul's Conversion	Acts 9:1–9	The Road to Damascus
AD 35–39	Travels to Damascus	Acts 9:6–10	
	Paul visits Arabia	Galatians 1:17	
	Returns to Damascus	Galatians 1:17, Acts 9:20–25	
AD 38	First visit to Jerusalem	Acts 9:26–29, Galatians 1:18	
	Paul travels to Tarsus	Acts 9:30, Galatians 1:21	
AD 45	Second visit to Jerusalem	Acts 11:17–30	
AD 46–48	First Apostolic Journey	Acts 13:1–14:28	Cyprus and Galatia
	Aid sent to Jerusalem	Acts 11:29–30	
	Sent out Barnabas	Acts 13:2–3	
	Ministry in Antioch, Iconium, Lystra and Derbe	Acts 13:14–14:23	
AD 49	Third visit to Jerusalem	Acts 15:1–29, Galatians 2:1	Jerusalem Council
AD 49–52	Second Apostolic Journey	Acts 15:40–18:22	Galatia, Macedonia, Greece, Asia Minor
AD 49	Wrote the letter to the Galatians		
	Joined by Timothy	Acts 16:1–5	
	Macedonian vision	Acts 16:6–10	
	In prison in Philippi with Silas	Acts 16:16–40	
	Ministry in Thessalonica, Berea, Athens, Corinth	Acts 17:1–18:17	
AD 51	Wrote two letters to the Thessalonians		

Date	Event	Reference	Comments
AD 53–57	Third Apostolic Journey	Acts 18:23–21:14	Galatia, Asia Minor, Macedonia, Greece
	Riot in Ephesus	Acts 19:21–41	
	Ministry in Macedonia, Greece, Troas	Acts 20:1–12	
	Exhorts the Ephesian elders	Acts 20:15–38	
AD 54	Wrote the first letter to the Corinthians		
AD 55	Wrote the second letter to the Corinthians		
AD 56	Wrote the letter to the Romans		
AD 57–59	Arrest in Jerusalem	Acts 21:15–26, 32	Trials and Imprisonment in Caesarea
	Before Governor Felix	Acts 24:1–27	
	Before Governor Festus	Acts 25:1–12	
	Before King Agrippa	Acts 25:22–26:32	
AD 60–63	Voyage to Rome	Acts 27:1–28:31	Roman Imprisonment
AD 61–63	Wrote letters to Ephesians, Philippians, Colossians, Philemon		
	Preaches two years in rented house	Acts 28:30–31	
AD 63–67	Release and Further Work		
AD 64	Wrote the first letter to Timothy		
AD 65	Wrote the letter to Titus		
AD 67	Final Imprisonment Wrote second letter to Timothy		
AD 68	Second Roman Imprisonment and Death		Martyrdom under Nero

The Christian message was spreading throughout the then-known world. A fisherman in the town of Capernaum finally ended up in Ephesus, away from his birthplace. Other disciples and converts were taking the Gospel to the world. While the sacrificial worship system was about to become obsolete forever, the Holy Spirit was empowering those who were accepting the Messiah, Jesus Christ, the One whom the Jews rejected.

The Destruction of the Temple

Herod's Temple was the centre of Israelite life and soon became the national focal point of the Jews as they carried out their religious festivals with much enthusiasm. The Sanhedrin, the highest court of Jewish law, convened within the walls of this place. There were also four religious groups, similar to four political powers, all fighting for supremacy: the Essenes, Pharisees, Sadducees, and the Zealots. Each had its agenda, and much infighting took place amongst the four groups.

The Essenes were a pious, exclusive group who believed in the soul living in the afterlife. They abstained from Temple worship and were opposed to the corrupt teaching taught. They devoted much of their time to studying and were stricter than the Pharisees regarding the Sabbath.

The Pharisees were the most popular sect in Judea, as they were involved in government, community, and religious practices. They believed in a combination of fate, free will, and that the soul is indestructible. In the afterlife, the Pharisees believed that the evil person would be punished for their sins and the good rewarded, so they acted accordingly. As community members, they focused on fellowship meals and followed the written and oral Torah. This group did not live peacefully with the Sadducees.

The Sadducees were drawn from priestly, aristocratic, and military circles, as they were often accused of being boorish and rude at times in their pursuit of wealth and higher social standing. They believed that God is not actively involved with the world and far removed from evil and that human beings have complete free will. They dismissed the idea of a soul living after death and punishment in the next world, so they rejected Oral law and focused instead on Temple worship.

The Zealots had a passion for liberty as they showed a real zeal for God, who must act on behalf of God, or the Lord will punish the whole nation. Zealots would kill or root out all offenders and were famous for doing their killing with a dagger.

At the time of the revolt and the siege, Jerusalem was not unified under a single leader but was home to several Jewish factions outlined previously. The Zealots, militant nationalists, played a significant role in initiating the revolt against Rome, while the Pharisees, who were experts in Jewish law and had a significant religious following, along with the Sadducees, due to the lack of unity and infighting among these groups, contributed to the difficulty in mounting a cohesive defence against the Romans.

Emperor Vespasian appointed his son Titus to end the rebellion by the Jews. In the spring of AD 70, Titus gathered his forces around Jerusalem. The Romans were well-equipped and experienced, having been engaged in the Jewish Revolt for several years. Inside the city, the Jewish defenders were in a state of disarray due to infighting among different factions. Despite this, they had prepared for the siege by storing food and fortifying the city's walls.

Jerusalem's geographical position on high ground and its formidable fortifications presented a significant challenge to the Roman attackers. When attempts failed to breach the city walls, a different tactic was used and so forced the city into submission through starvation. As food and water supply dwindled and disease spread among the inhabitants, infighting among the Jewish factions also continued, further weakening the city's defences.

In the summer of AD 70, the Romans finally managed to breach the Third Wall, then the Second, and finally penetrated the heavily fortified First Wall, entering the Upper City, where they massacred the remaining population and destroyed Herod's Temple.

The spring of AD 70 would have aligned with Passover and could have brought thoughts of their ancestors as they were delivered from death when the Lord passed over them, and they embraced a new life as God's chosen people. But history records a different outcome as the once chosen people, because of their continued disobedience to the covenant they had agreed to so many years previous, are returned to bondage.

By the summer, which could align with the fourth feast, Feast of Weeks or Pentecost, the Jews were very aware, as a nation, that many had been killed or returned to slavery as their glorious temple lay in ruins and their religious sacrificial system forever removed. They were the chosen, but because of bad attitudes, fraught with the self-focus of those who were doing all things right in their own eyes, they paid the price.

Jewish tradition recalls that on Yom Kippa, the High Priest tied a crimson wool thread around the horns of the scapegoat and sent him off into the wilderness accompanied by a priest. The priest escorted the scapegoat for twelve miles to a designated place where he pushed the goat over a cliff, symbolically bearing Israel's sins. A portion of the crimson thread was attached to the door of the temple before the goat was sent into the wilderness. When the goat was pushed off the cliff and died, the thread on the door at the temple was said to turn from red to white.

This was seen as a divine sign to the people that God had accepted their sacrifice and their sins were forgiven. The sign was based on Isaiah 1:18, which says, *"Though your sins are as scarlet, they will be as white as snow; though they are red like crimson, they will be like wool."* Rabbinic writings tell us that for forty years before the destruction of the temple, the thread stopped turning white.

With these thoughts in mind, a blind songwriter by the name of Fanny Crosby wrote the following words.

Though your sins be as scarlet,
They shall be as white as snow;
Though they be red like crimson,
They shall be as wool;
Though your sins be as scarlet,
They shall be as white as snow.

Hear the voice that entreats you,
O return ye unto God!
He is of great compassion,
And of wondrous love;
Hear the voice that entreats you,
O return ye unto God!

He'll forgive your transgressions,
And remember them no more;
"Look unto Me, ye people,"
Saith the Lord your God;
He'll forgive your transgressions,
And remember them no more.

Public Domain

The rebellion against Rome in 66 AD changed the Jewish lifestyle forever, as the Temple was destroyed in 70 AD. Those who were not killed were taken as slaves, with many sent to the mines of Egypt or sold in slave markets. The city of Jerusalem was thoroughly sacked by the Romans, as buildings, homes, and walls were torn down, leaving the city in ruins. The Romans also carried off the treasures of the Temple as spoils of war, including the Menorah, which was famously depicted on the Arch of Titus in Rome.

With the destruction of the temple, the practice of Judaism had to adapt, necessitating a major shift in religious practice and thought, leading to the development of Rabbinic Judaism. The destruction of Jerusalem also had a profound impact on the early Christian movement, as many followers of Jesus had fled the city before the siege, spreading their beliefs to other parts of the Roman Empire.

Jesus warned that the Temple would be destroyed, and some saw the destruction of the Temple and Jerusalem as the prophetic fulfilment of his warning. Without a central Jewish authority in Jerusalem and with Jewish communities scattered, Christianity began to evolve as a distinct religion, increasingly separate from its Jewish roots. The sacrificial system had been abolished as Jesus was the sacrificial Lamb who became our Great High Priest.

The Pharisees were the only group to recover from the destruction and developed the rabbinic movement, which eventually became the normal tradition of Judaism, as prayer took the place of sacrifice, and worship was rebuilt around rabbis who acted as teachers and leaders of individual communities. For Jews, the synagogue became the bridge between the loss of their worship centre and the hope for the rebuilding of a Temple.

Many Jews were sold into slavery, especially to work in the mines of the Egyptians. As about fifteen hundred years had passed from Moses leading the Hebrews out of slavery and oppression, the Hebrews had come full circle and returned to Egypt and slavery. The Lord refined this wayward people, but grumbling and disobedience were their undoing. Instead of awareness of the Lord as their guide and helper, they chose to be like everyone else.

The children of Israel had received the three promises and seen them fulfilled, but at the last hurdle, they chose to reject the Messiah, who would lead them to the real Promise Land, now, they returned to their wanderings in the desert experienced by their ancestors. They would wander the earth until the return of Jesus, and then their eternal fate would be determined.

As the Jews continued to observe the Feasts, as no blood sacrifice was carried out, no atonement was available. Their belief is now that forgiveness of sin is obtained through repentance, prayer, and good deeds. They now concentrate on the works of man, not on the works that Jesus completed for us in His lived life, death and resurrection. As Jesus said:

> *"Therefore I said that you will die in your sins;*
> *for if you do not believe that I am He,*
> *you will die in your sins."*

John 8:24

During Jesus' Galilean ministry, in association with the Sermon on the Mount, Jesus taught about the task that was set for Him to fulfil. No one would have understood that He was prophesying about the future and His involvement. When addressing the crowds, Jesus said:

> *"Do not think that I came to destroy*
> *the Law or the Prophets.*
> *I did not come to destroy but to fulfil.*
> *For assuredly, I say to you,*
> *till heaven and earth pass away,*
> *one jot or one tittle will by no means pass*
> *from the law till all is fulfilled."*
>
> Matthew 5:17–18

When Jesus, the sinless, spotless Son of God, the sacrificial Lamb, died for our sins, the Old Covenant ceased, and the New Covenant took its place. The Law and the sacrificial system contained within the Law were replaced with Grace. Jesus fulfilled what Father God required for the redemption of man, to once again have fellowship with Him. The sinless life lived by Jesus, laying down His own life by taking it up again to be resurrected from the dead, enabled Jesus to become our Great High Priest.

Because Jesus had fulfilled all the requirements, when we accept Him as our Lord and Saviour, the Law has no hold on us and has passed away, as we, the redeemed, are accepted into the New Covenant through Grace. Jesus did not destroy the Law or the Prophets, as when Moses, representing the Law, and Elijah, representing the Prophets, met with Jesus at the Transfiguration (Matthew 17:1–8), all was in place for Jesus to proceed and fulfil them both.

Second Temple Timeline

Date	Comment
573 BC	The Prophet Ezekiel, when in Babylonian exile, had a vision of a magnificent Temple. (Ezekiel 40–48).
539 BC	Babylonian king Belshazzar desecrates the temple vessels at pagan feast. (Daniel 5:1–4). Persian monarch Cyrus the Great conquers Babylon.
538 BC	Cyrus issues a decree allowing Jews in exile to return to Jerusalem and rebuild the city and the Temple, and returns Temple vessels taken by Nebuchadnezzar (2 Chron. 36:22–23; Ezra 1:1–11; 6:3–15).
520–515 BC	Zerubbabel, a descendant of David, rebuilds and dedicates the Temple and restores the sacrificial system (Ezra 3:1–13; 5:1–17; 6:1–18).
445 BC	Nehemiah returns to Jerusalem from Persia to rebuild the walls of the city and protect the Temple Mount (Nehemiah 1 – 7:4).
332 BC	Alexander the Great conquers Jerusalem but spares the Temple.
175 BC	Antiochus IV Epiphanes, king of Syria, plunders the Temple.
168 BC	Different Jewish writings including the 'Dead Sea Scrolls' are produced and include prophesies about the restoration of the Temple.
167 BC	The soldiers of Antiochus defile the Temple. Jewish sacrifices are stopped and the worship of the Olympian Zeus is instituted.
164 BC	Judas Maccabeus restores Jewish ritual by cleansing and rededicating the Temple after a successful revolt.
67 BC	Aristobulus besieges Jerusalem. The family war between Aristobulus and Hyrcanus led to the intervention of Rome and the end of Jewish independence.
63 BC	Roman emperor Pompey conquers Jerusalem and enters the Holy of Holies.
20–18 BC	Herod the Great rebuilt the Temple and worship was restored.
70 AD	Jerusalem and the Temple destroyed by the Roman Commander Titus. Many Jews killed and the remnant exiled.

The Observance of Passover Today

Today, the Passover is still celebrated in Jewish homes, without the sacrifice of a lamb. It has developed since the time of Jesus to an elaborate ceremony extended by the Rabbis in the 15th century AD, designed to both remember the Hebrews' escape from slavery in Egypt and to teach the community, especially children, the Jewish heritage.

Some Christians also celebrate Passover as a once-a-year meal following the Seder or order designed by Jewish rabbis. Most Christians also remember Jesus' last meal with His disciples with a simple Communion or Eucharist in the weekly church service. This practice reminds us of Jesus' sacrifice on the cross, replacing the lamb sacrificed by the Rabbis under the Old Covenant.

The question to be asked is, "What happened to the Passover between Jesus' Resurrection and the destruction of the Temple in AD 70?" Between AD 33 and AD70, the Jewish community continued to hold annual Passover celebrations with the sacrifices performed by the Priests.

However, when Jerusalem and the Temple were destroyed by the invading Roman Army in AD 70, animal sacrifice was no longer practised. Passover changed again, for without the shedding of blood, there was no remission of sins. The practice of Judaism had to adapt, necessitating a major shift in religious practice and thought, leading to the development of a Rabbinic Judaism movement, which eventually became the normal tradition of Judaism. Prayer took the place of sacrifice, and worship was revised as the rabbis acted as teachers and leaders of individual communities. For Jews, the synagogue became the bridge between the loss of their worship centre and the hope for the rebuilding of a Temple.

Most Jews follow the Jewish religious practices, similar to many people not being Christians, but there is always a remnant who discover the truth by the grace of God. When Jesus was arrested and stood before Caiaphas in front of the Sanhedrin, He was asked the question, *"Are You the Christ, the Son of the Blessed?"* (Mark 14:61b). Jesus answered truthfully with the words, *"Yes, I am"* (v62a). When Jesus answered their question, the religious leaders did not accept His answer but chose to charge Him with blasphemy, as this suited their purpose.

Apart from a remnant of Jews who have converted to Christianity, most Jews today ignore the answer Jesus gave when asked if He was the Messiah, the rest ignored the answer that Jesus gave confirming that He was the expected Messiah, the leader they were anticipating. He wasn't what they saw as a conquering hero, but a person from the tribe of Judah, not a Levite, who had nothing to offer them but pain and suffering in their world of fraud and false teaching.

As the Jews continued the sacrificial practices between AD 33 and AD 70, the Christians began remembering Jesus' last meal when they gathered. Paul, when writing his first letter to the Corinthians, said:

> *"Purge out the old leaven,*
> *that you may be a new lump,*
> *since you truly are unleavened.*
> *For indeed Christ, our Passover,*
> *was sacrificed for us."*

1 Corinthians 5:7

We are not told how the early Christians celebrated Passover, but Paul, in his writings, provided us with a glimpse of how and what they did when he wrote:

> *"When you come together in one place,*
> *it is not to eat the Lord's Supper.*
> *For in eating, each one takes*
> *his own supper ahead of others;*
> *and one is hungry and another is drunk."*

1 Corinthians 11:21

Paul, in his teaching, corrected their wrong attitudes and practices that he had received from the Lord when he wrote:

> *"The Lord Jesus on the same night*
> *in which He was betrayed took bread;*
> *and when He had given thanks,*
> *He broke it and said,*
> *'Take, eat, this is My body which is broken for you;*
> *do this in remembrance of Me.'*
> *In the same manner He took also the cup after supper,*
> *saying, 'This is the new covenant in My blood.*
> *This do, as often as you drink it,*
> *in remembrance of Me'."*
>
> 1 Corinthians 11:24–25

Paul, throughout his ministry, continued to go to the Jews first and then the Gentiles. After preaching and teaching for many years, Luke records the efforts of Paul in about AD 48 when he says:

> *"Then Paul and Barnabas grew bold and said,*
> *'It was necessary that the word of God*
> *should be spoken to you first;*
> *but since you reject it,*
> *and judge yourselves unworthy of everlasting life,*
> *behold, we turn to the Gentiles'."*
>
> Acts 13:46

In about AD 52, Luke writes that Paul was still convicted he was required to share the gospel with the Jews, so he continued but was rejected a second time as Luke wrote:

> *"But when they opposed him and blasphemed,*
> *he shook his garments and said to them,*
> *'Your blood be upon your own heads;*
> *I am clean.*
> *From now on I will go to the Gentiles'."*

Acts 18:6

Paul's ministry finally took him to Rome, about AD 61, where he rented a home and preached to the Jews, who greatly disputed among themselves about the subject matter Paul was preaching and teaching. Paul finally conceded that he had completed his mission to the Jews, as Luke recorded:

> *"Therefore let it be known to you*
> *that the salvation of God*
> *has been sent to the Gentiles,*
> *and they will hear it!"*

Acts 28:28

While many Jews were focusing on the past *'Laws of Moses'* and what was to be observed regarding the feasts and customs, Paul, in his last years, wrote the following:

"Brethren, I do not count myself to have apprehended;
but one thing I do,
forgetting those things which are behind
and reaching forward to those things which are ahead,
I press toward the goal for the prize
of the upward call of God in Christ Jesus."

Philippians 3:13–14

The question is still being asked today and rejected, "Are You the Messiah?" Paul was suggesting, because the New Covenant was in place, *"Old things have passed away; behold, all things have become new"* (1 Corinthians 5:17b). As keeping the Law was impossible for the Jews, the covenant of Grace had replaced the Law, along with sacrificial worship. The Jews, as well as the early Christians, could remember the feasts but were under no obligation to keep them, but remember the excellent work completed by Jesus and give all the praise to Father God.

While it is great to enjoy and remember the things of the past and to learn from our mistakes, it is another to hold them in awe and reverence and never accept the lessons to be learned. While Passover is a great story about a people whom God led out of suffering and oppression to be His people to worship Him, the fact that they disobeyed His commands and grumbled is overlooked.

Have we learnt anything from the past? God spoke into existence a world where people would worship Him, but this turned sour when sin entered into His garden through Eve and then Adam. A remnant still worshipped God until the Lord presented Abram with three promises that would give Father God a covenant people to worship Him. But this again failed, as the covenanted people rejected His Son, so another solution was brought to the table. Selected Gentiles along with Jews. We know this is true because Jesus said:

> *"You did not choose Me,*
> *but I chose you and appointed you*
> *that you should go and bear fruit,*
> *and that your fruit should remain,*
> *that whatever you ask the Father*
> *in My name He may give you."*
>
> John 15:16

Through the introduction of Grace and the Holy Spirit, the way was opened once more for *'The Called'* to inherit the kingdom of God. When Father God is ready, and He has all His chosen people who will worship continually for all eternity, Father God will finally have His way. Only those who have accepted Jesus Christ as their personal Lord and Saviour will be granted entrance into the Kingdom of Heaven.

Saul/Paul was blind to the way of salvation until his Damascus road experience (Acts 9:1–19), where he received light and fresh understanding. Many in the past and today required an awakening that only the Holy Spirit can bring. While wisdom is given to those who ask Father God (James 1:5), understanding can only be obtained through the Holy Spirit. Jesus, when asked about the purpose of parables, said:

> *"I speak to them in parables,*
> *because seeing they do not see,*
> *and hearing they do not hear,*
> *nor do they understand."*

Matthew 13:13

It has been said that if you want to hide something, put it in plain sight. So, how does this apply to many reluctant Jews and those who are part of the promises given to Abram? What were the promises given so many years ago?

> *"I will make you a great nation;*
> *I will bless you and make your name great;*
> *and you shall be a blessing."*

Genesis 12:2

The promises were given to Abram, who later became Abraham and to his descendants. You would remember that Abraham had eight sons, not just one, Isaac. Ishmael was the first son Abraham had with Hagar. Isaac was the second son Abram had with Sarah. Because Haggar was a slave, Ishmael represented the Law, whereas Isaac was a child of the covenant and represented Grace.

Here, we have the golden thread that runs right through the Bible: that of Law and Grace. From the two trees in the middle of the Garden of Eden, the tree of the knowledge of good and evil and the tree of life (Genesis 2:9b), to the Book of Revelation.

Ishmael's family grew and eventually became the Muslims who follow Allah, not Father God, pay homage to Mohammad, not Jesus, and have their own scriptures, the Qur'an, and Shari Law, as they live under the Law. Their main worship centres are Mecca, Medina and Jerusalem. In Jerusalem, their Mosque was built over the site of Solomon's Temple, which later became Herod's Temple.

The one remaining part of Herod's Temple is the Wailing Wall, where many Orthodox Jews gather to pray as they remember the destruction of their temple and pray for the rebuilding of a new temple for them to once more establish sacrificial worship and the feasts. Ishmael's descendants chose Mohammad and the Shari Law, whereas Isaac's descendants rejected Jesus and forfeited Grace.

I see a parallel between the Mosque and the Wailing Wall. The Law dominates the Temple Mount and the worship of Allah, where the wailing wall is for those who should be crying out to God for repentance, not justice. Jesus said, *"Seeing they shall not see and hearing they will not understand."*

Jesus shared and taught an alternative for those who have chosen to live under the Law when He said:

> *"Come unto Me,*
> *all you who labour and are heavy laden,*
> *and I will give you rest.*
> *Take My yoke upon you and learn from Me,*
> *for I am gentle and lowly in heart,*
> *and you will find rest for your souls.*
> *For My yoke is easy and My burden is light."*
>
> Matthew 11:28–30

Living under the New Covenant of Grace, which Jesus instigated, removed the burden of the Law, as the Law was replaced with further understanding for those who would be part and join themselves to the body of Christ. Jesus shared on another occasion what His burden entailed when He said:

> *"Hear, O Israel, the Lord our God,*
> *the Lord is one.*
> *'And you shall love the Lord your God*
> *with all your heart, with all your soul,*

> *with all your mind,*
> *and with all your strength'.*
> *This is the first commandment.*
> *And the second, like it, is this:*
> *'You shall love your neighbour as yourself'.*
> *There is no other commandment*
> *greater than these."*
>
> Mark 12:29b–31

A Modern Christian Passover

Christians who choose to follow the Jewish practice of Passover can use a service as outlined here. The Passover remembrance is called the Haggadah, which means 'Go Forth and Learn'. A special Seder Plate is used to display the various items of food that represent the Passover story to be shared. While no lamb is slaughtered between the evenings, other parts are symbolised to represent the Exodus story as it is retold to all those who have gathered for the Passover Remembrance Meal.

During the first Passover, the Hebrews sat inside a home with blood applied to the door posts, sharing a meal, fully dressed, eating roasted lamb accompanied with unleavened bread and bitter herbs, as the Lord passed over the Hebrews, whereas today, the celebration is more elaborate. At least the Passover has returned to a family celebration. I have chosen to use what appears to be a basic Christian Haggadah with some explanations attached to each step.

Blessing the Wine

Open with a prayer, thanking God for freeing us from slavery, both through the Exodus from Egypt and from sin through our Messiah.

First Hand-Washing

Pass the washing bowl around, and each participant should wash and dry their hands, as this signifies that we must approach God with clean hands and a pure heart.

The Vegetables

Dip the parsley in salt water as you tell the participants that this reminds us of the shed tears in slavery. Eat it after the leader has praised God for the vegetables.

Breaking the Matzah

The leader removes the middle piece of matzah from the three pieces of matzah that have been set aside. It should be broken in two, and the larger piece should be wrapped in the cloth. In some homes, it is hidden somewhere in the house for the children to find later, as this reminds us that Jesus was broken, wrapped, and buried.

The Observance of Passover Today

Telling the Story

The leader tells the Passover story. During this part, as the plagues are recalled, the participants dip their finger in the wine and drop a drop of wine onto a piece of matzah as each plague is recalled (blood, frogs, lice, flies, livestock, boils, hail, locusts, darkness, and the death of the firstborn). The leader should emphasise the actual Passover part of the story (lamb's blood on the doorpost saving God's people) and that Jesus' blood allowed our exodus from the slavery of our sin.

Second Hand-Washing

Pass the washing bowl around, and each participant should wash and dry their hands. This reinforces the significance that we must approach God with clean hands and a pure heart.

First Blessing on Matzah

Each person should hold up a piece of matzah. The leader should again say that we eat matzah because the Israelites left with no time for their bread to rise. The matzah is also like Jesus, who wasn't 'leavened' with sin so that He could be a sacrifice for us.

Second Blessing on Matzah

The leader should show the horseradish and tell everyone that this reminds us of the bitterness of slavery. The leader should explain that the charoset reminds us of the mortar used by the Israelite slaves to build brick buildings for the Egyptians.

The Bitter Herbs

The leader should praise God for the reminder of the bitter herbs and then invite all participants to put some horseradish on their matzah.

The Wine

Everyone lifts the second cup of wine as the leader praises God for saving us and for the fruit of the vine. Then everyone should drink and eat the matzah.

The Festive Meal

The leader thanks God for the food and for this time to remember the Passover and Jesus, our 'Passover Lamb'. The meal is now served.

Grace after Meals

After the meal is the third cup of wine, as you'll recognise this part from the Last Supper recorded in the Gospels. If the middle matzah was hidden, now is the time to find it. The leader breaks the once-hidden broken matzah into pieces and gives each believer at the table a piece. Another glass of wine is poured, and everyone should hold the matzah and wine. The leader should summarise the Last Supper and then quote 1 Corinthians 11:24 and Mark 14:22, where Jesus said, *"Take, eat; this is My body which is broken for you; do this in remembrance of Me."* Then, everyone should eat their piece of matzah but hold their cup of wine. The leader should then quote 1 Corinthians 11:25 and Mark 14:24, where Jesus said, *"This cup is the new covenant in my blood. This do, as often as you drink it, in remembrance of Me."* Then, all believers should drink the third cup.

Hymns of Praise

This is usually the time for a song of praise. Some say a Psalm or sing a hymn.

The Fourth Cup

The leader now pours the fourth cup of wine, praises God for the fruit of the vine, and everyone drinks it.

Concluding Thoughts

The leader concludes, reminding everyone that tonight's feast is a reminder of God's deliverance for us, not only from slavery in Egypt but also from our sin and the death we deserve. We are redeemed through the blood of Jesus, just as the blood of the lamb in the first Passover redeemed the Israelites.

The mainstream Jews are still wandering in the desert places. Let us thank Father God for the remnant who are part of *'The Called'*.

The Marriage Supper of the Lamb

> *"But I say to you,*
> *I will not drink of this fruit of the vine*
> *from now until that day when I drink it new*
> *with you in My Father's kingdom."*
>
> Matthew 26:29

How does the Marriage Supper of the Lamb become a Passover? To be a participant in the first Passover, Egypt represented the world and the worship of many gods, whereas Goshen was the place that represented the church or those who have accepted the Lord Jesus Christ as their own personal Saviour. Just as there could have been those who did not obey the commands of Moses in Goshen, so in the church today, for some, it is just a social club

Each Hebrew male was required to carry in his body the mark of separation as allegiance to Father God through circumcision. Paul refers to us all carrying in our bodies the marks of acceptance, including females.

> *"From now on let no one trouble me,*
> *for I bear in my body*
> *the marks of the Lord Jesus Christ."*
>
> Galatians 6:17, 2 Corinthians 11:23–27

It has been said that scars are the marks of healed wounds. James, the earthly brother of Jesus, told us to expect various trials but to count it all joy (James 1:2). John, when writing words of encouragement to the faithful, said:

> *"Because you have kept My command to persevere,*
> *I also will keep you from the hour of trial*
> *which shall come upon the whole world,*
> *to test those who dwell on the earth."*
>
> Revelation 3:10

As committed followers of Jesus, washed in the blood of the Lamb, we are forgiven and found righteous in the eyes of Father God. Judgement day will not concern us, as our relationship with the Father enables the invited guests to accompany the Groom and enjoy fellowship with all who have accepted, been patient, persisted, and persevered, waiting expectantly for His return, weathering the storms of life.

On the eve of the first Passover, the children of Israel, His separated people, were required to be dressed and ready to leave when told as they ate the meal of roast lamb, bitter herbs and unleavened bread. Around midnight, the Lord passed through the land and killed the firstborn, who were not covered by the blood of the lamb on the doorposts and lentil.

The Israelites left their homes with their earthly possessions and made their way out of the city, following Moses in an orderly fashion to the promised land. They had no idea how long this journey would take, but in faith, they followed Moses as he had the words of the Lord.

The question that needs to be asked is, "How does what the Hebrews carried out in obedience apply to us and the Passover?" Jesus said, *"You did not choose Me, but I chose you and appointed you that you might go and bear (support) fruit, and that your fruit should remain, that whatever you ask the Father in My name He may give you."* John 15:16

Just as the children of Israel were chosen, Jesus came to seek and save the lost, which is where you and I come in. Once we have applied the shed blood of Jesus to our life, we are covered from spiritual death or should be.

All through our yielded life to Christ, we participated at the table that the Lord prepared for us in the presence of our enemies (Psalm 23: 5a). We are dressed in the Armour of God, waiting for the call to vacate this earthly home. As all of our earthly possessions will be left behind, what we take with us are those treasures that have been previously laid up or stored in heaven. Matthew 6:19–21

We of the called follow Jesus to the place He has prepared for us, but we need to pass through the *'Red Sea'*, or the *'Valley of the shadow of death'*, which is the way to the Promised Land. How the children of Israel walked through towering water on both sides could have looked like a valley when, at any time, the waters could have returned, but the Lord was true to His word and provided a way. The passage through was just a shadow, meaning there was nothing to fear while the Lord was present.

We are told in the Bible that it is appointed for men to die once, but after this, the judgement (Hebrews 9:27). We have no idea what we will be presented with between this life and the next. Some have said, "Absent from the body, present with the Lord." But there is always an in-between, no matter how small the gap. David assured us that there is nothing to fear as the valley contains only a shadow of death and is of no concern to us, as Jesus accompanies *'The Called'* with His rod and staff, which bring comfort to us. Psalm 23:4

Paul, when writing his second letter to the Thessalonians, warned about sitting around idle, waiting for Jesus to return, but to be busy with the Lord's work.

> *"For we hear that there are some who walk*
> *among you in a disorderly manner,*
> *not working at all, but are busybodies.*

> *But as for you, brethren,*
> *do not grow weary in doing good."*
>
> 2 Thessalonians 3:11–13

The Feast of Trumpets has sounded, and we are summonsed to leave this earth, and everyone whose names are written in the Lamb's Book of Life stands before the Judgement Bar of Father God. The rest have been dispatched to the Lake of Fire after having knelt and acknowledged Jesus as Lord. The Lord gave fair warning to those who chose to go their way and do their own thing, ignoring the prompting of the Holy Spirit, for it is written:

> *"Do not fear those who kill the body*
> *but cannot kill the soul.*
> *But rather fear Him*
> *who is able to destroy*
> *both body and soul in hell."*
>
> Matthew 10:28

Jesus will summon *'the Called'* — those who have followed the promptings of the Holy Spirit — to be with Him. Many who believe they should be invited will also want to attend as they have pursued 'works' as their entitlement to the Marriage Supper.

> *"They will come from the east and the west,*
> *from the north and the south,*
> *and sit down in the kingdom of God."*
>
> Luke 13:29

The books are then opened, and we are judged for adherence to the promptings given to us throughout the life we were given by the revealed will of Father God. This is where a further separation takes place as the sheep are separated from the goats, like Gideon, when he selected the three hundred, not thousands, only those worthy and alert to fight for the Lord (Judges 7:4–7). For the Lord will say to the thousands:

> *"Depart from Me, you cursed,*
> *into the everlasting fire*
> *prepared for the devil and his angels:*
> *for I was hungry and you gave Me no food;*
> *I was thirsty and you gave me no drink;*
> *I was a stranger and you did not take Me in,*
> *naked and you did not clothe Me,*
> *sick and in prison, and you did not visit Me."*
>
> Matthew 25:41–43

This was foretold by Jesus during His earthly ministry when He told the following Parable.

> *"But when the king came in to see the guests, he saw a man there who did not have on a wedding garment. Then the king said to the servants, 'Bind him hand and foot, take him away, and cast him into outer darkness; there will be weeping and gnashing of teeth'."*
> Matthew 22:11–13

> *"Many are called but few are choice."*
>
> Matthew 22:14

Once the preparation for the supper has been completed, the door will be shut forever, and only those found worthy will attend the last Passover with the Lord, or the Marriage Supper of the Lamb, where Jesus will invite all those present to join with Him as we participate in His feast, as He drinks the fourth *'Cup of Praise'*. This will be a joyous occasion as only those of *'the Called'* along with the Angels, will sing praise and honour to the King of Kings.

Only because of the New Covenant are we able to attend, as under the Old Covenant, the Law, we should die.

> *"And it is appointed for men to die once,*
> *but after this the judgment, so*
> *Christ was offered once to bear the sins of many,*
> *to those who eagerly wait for Him*
> *He will appear a second time,*
> *apart from sin, for salvation."*
>
> Hebrews 9:27–28

We have passed from physical and spiritual death to spiritual life, as the Passover represents our life and how we listen and react to the promptings of the Holy Spirit. The Holy Spirit calls us to leave the life we knew and follow Him in obedience to the Promised Land, where Jesus has already prepared a place for us. John 14:2

As we accept the Holy Spirit's call on our life, we are subject to the law of God, but because of what Jesus completed on our behalf, grace is offered to cover our sin. Our every day is a refinement from where we were to the place the Lord has called us to be. He enabled us to pass through the pruning process (John 15:1–8) and, under His guidance, accept what has happened to us, although we may not understand until much later.

While we can expect many trials and temptations, grumbling about where the Lord has allowed us to go is never an option. Although the way appears hard, trust in His unfailing love will continue to be our companion. We have the assurance that He will never leave or forsake us and that He will guide every step we take as we follow His lead.

The Lord has given us guidelines to follow in His word. Isaiah outlined these for us under the heading, *'The Fast God Requires'* (Isaiah 58:6–13). When fulfilling what is written, blessings follow, but if neglected, disobedience has its reward. Two observations to share is to make sure we keep the Sabbath as a Holy Day, not doing our own thing (v13a). The other is only to speak what the Holy Spirit instructs us to say, not using our own words (v13b).

Many feast days are provided for us as we worship Him in spirit and truth. Every seventh day is a Sabbath, and at other times, we only require two or three to be present in His name, for the presence of the Lord to be in our midst. Even on dark days, He prepares a table with food catered to our needs, not our wants.

As we walk daily with the Shepherd, we are assured of His love and protection in every situation. Our walk is all about Him and not about us because our life is in the being, not in the doing. We should never recoil when told to proceed, for if we do, we may not enter the Promised Land as so many of the children of Israel found out.

As we begin in *'Faith'*, of which a portion has been given to us, we progress in our walk with Him to a *'Hope'* in Jesus. Because He *'Loves'* us and was willing to give His life to cover our sins, to redeem us from all unrighteousness, we *'Trust'* His every word and follow all His commands obediently and faithfully, which assures us of His *'Peace'* which surpasses all understanding.

Because we are *'the Called'*, we have been chosen to be present at the last Passover, the marriage Feast with the Lamb, where our soul and spirit will be clothed in righteousness, in the presence of our Lord and Saviour, Jesus Christ. Amen.

Part 2

The Journey of the Tabernacle

The Tabernacle of Meeting

The Tabernacle had a journey all of its own, which only when studied, revealed much to the inquirer's mind. As I gazed at a picture of the Garden of Eden, which contained the *'Tree of Life'*, then in front, the *'Tree of the Knowledge of Good and Evil'*, a river proceeded from the two trees and split into four rivers. On each side of the main river were cherubim with a flaming sword to keep the way to the *'Tree of Life'*. Genesis 2:9

With this picture firmly planted in my mind, I gazed at another picture; this one was of the Tabernacle in all its glory and splendour. As I looked intently at the image before me, my eyes were drawn to the curtain that covered the entrance or the 'Door' into the Tabernacle. The heavy curtain was adorned with cherubim. As I looked further to the curtain that separated the 'Holy Place' from the 'Most Holy Place' or 'Holy of Holies', again I noticed the cherubim that adorned the separation curtain.

Just as cherubim guarded the way to the *'Tree of Life'* in the Garden of Eden, the cherubim on the curtains of the Tabernacle were a constant reminder to the priests who would venture into the sanctuary and the Lord's presence that they were to be Holy, with clean hands and a pure heart. The cherubim guarded the way into the Tabernacle and the 'Holy of Holies'.

> *"Who may ascend into the hill of the Lord?*
> *Or who may stand in His holy place?*
> *He who has clean hands and a pure heart,*
> *Who has not lifted up his soul to an idol,*
> *nor sworn deceitfully."*
>
> Psalm 24:3–4

My mind went into overdrive as my thoughts took me to another place. The Tabernacle was modelled on the 'Garden of Eden'.

The Lord had planted, not created, a garden in the east of Eden and all the other created beings lived outside the Garden. The Lord had placed the Tabernacle in the middle of the children of Israel, who camped around the Tabernacle. The Lord had placed cherubim on the entrance to the Tabernacle, just as the cherubim kept the way to the *'Tree of Life'* in the garden.

When you venture inside the Tabernacle through the 'Door', on the left is the 'Candelabra', and to the right is the 'Shewbread Table'. The 'Candelabra' represents the word of God, while the 'Shewbread Table' is a place where we can have communion with the Father. When both of these are coupled together, you have the *'Tree of the Knowledge of Good and Evil'*. This is not a bad tree, but a tree for us that is enlightening.

We go to the 'Candelabra' and search the word of God, and then take what we are given and go to the 'Shewbread Table', where we commune with Father God with the help of the Holy Spirit to obtain an answer. Jesus, when sharing His thoughts in the 'Sermon on the Mount' said:

> *"Ask and it will be given to you;*
> *seek, and you will find;*
> *knock, and it will be opened."*

Matthew 7:7

Solomon, when recording his thoughts many years previous to Jesus, said:

> *My son, pay attention to my wisdom;*
> *Lend your ear to my understanding,*
> *that you may preserve discretion,*
> *and your lips may keep knowledge."*

Proverbs 5:1–2

When both these verses are blended, the outcome opens the way.

"Ask for wisdom, and you will receive discretion.
Seek understanding, and you will receive knowledge."

What is before us is a two–step plan set out in scripture for the discerning soul. At the 'Candelabra', we ask and are told, *"Your word is a lamp to my feet and a light to my path"* (Psalm 119:105). As we have asked for wisdom (James 1:5), we have understanding. But what do we do we do with the understanding given to us? We seek direction from the Lord, which takes us to the 'Shewbread Table' where we commune and talk with the Lord through the Holy Spirit.

I am reminded of Jesus when He shared the 'Last Supper' with His disciples. They knew His teaching, as He had said:

"I am the bread of life.
He who comes to Me shall never be hungry,
and He who believes in Me shall never thrist."

John 6:35

As He took the bread, blessed and broke it, then distributed the segments to the eleven, He said:

"Take, eat;
this is My body which is broken for you;
do this in remembrance of Me."

In the same manner He also took the cup after supper, saying:

> *"This cup is the new covenant in My blood.*
> *This do, as often as you drink it,*
> *in remembrance of Me."*
>
> 1 Corinthians 11:24–25

As we eat and drink at the 'Shewbread Table,' we enjoy the benefits of a servant life given to our Lord and Master, Jesus Christ, who faithfully answers all our sincere needs. As we come to Jesus with our concerns, we feed on Him; then, because we believe, He provides us with spiritual living water to quench our thirst, just as Jesus told the woman at the well in Samaria.

> *"Whoever drinks of the water*
> *that I shall give him will never thirst.*
> *But the water that I shall give him*
> *will become in him a fountain of water*
> *springing up into everlasting life."*
>
> John 4:14

As we have the Word of God and the Bread of Life, we can proceed, as the way is open to the 'Incense Altar' where we make our petitions known to Father God through the Holy Spirit and the 'Holy of Holies', which is the *'Tree of Life'*. The Tabernacle interior is a representation of what the Lord had planted in the 'Garden of Eden', as the way is guarded by the cherubim, and both trees are there with the altar set before the Lord, who walks in the Garden and talks with those who belong to Him.

Jesus also taught us about the 'Garden of Eden' and the 'Tabernacle' when He said:

> *"I am the door.*
> *If anyone enters by Me, he will be saved,*
> *and go in and out and find pasture.*
> *The thief does not come except to steal,*
> *and to kill, and to destroy.*
> *I have come that they may have life,*
> *and that they may have it more abundantly."*
>
> John 10:9–10

Satan ventured into the planted garden in Eden as a thief who stole, killed, and destroyed. When the Tabernacle was built, the Lord put cherubim to guard the way into His presence. As the 'Good Shepherd' protects us with His rod and staff, we can have confidence that we are protected, as we rely on the power of the 'Name of Jesus' because of what He accomplished for us.

The Tabernacle of the Lord

When Moses was summoned to meet the Lord on Mount Sinai, he took Joshua with him. Joshua waited halfway up the mountain, and Moses ascended to the peak of the mountain, where he stayed for forty days. When Moses rejoined Joshua, who had patiently waited, he had two tablets of stone outlining the covenant the Lord had provided for the children of Israel who had previously agreed to follow. Exodus 19:8

As the two returned down the mountain, Joshua remarked to Moses:

"There is a noise of war in the camp."
But Moses replied,
"It is not the noise of the shout of victory,
Nor the noise of the cry of defeat,
but the sound of singing I hear."

Exodus 32:17b–18

When Moses saw the children of Israel worshipping the golden calf that Aaron had carved and set up, Moses threw the stone tablets, which broke into pieces, signifying that the children of Israel had broken the Lord's covenant. After Moses had interceded for the sin of the Israelites, he once again made his way into the presence of the Lord. Exodus 34:1

The Lord wrote down the Commandments and rules previously given to Moses regarding many aspects of relationships, sickness, feasts and worship.

Back in Egypt, there were many gods who each had their place for worship, but because the Israelites were worshipping the 'One True God', they only required one place for worship. The Lord gave instructions for the construction of a place where He could dwell among the Israelites and, in their presence, called the 'Tabernacle' or 'Tent of Meeting'.

Hebrew Trades

When the word Hebrew is mentioned, thousands of people making bricks for Egyptian buildings is first and foremost in our thinking, but these people were more than brick makers. Many were farmers who grew the crops and, when harvested, provided the straw to make the bricks. There were shepherds and those who kept cattle, along with many other skilled trades.

One could imagine that the Egyptians were the upper class and the rich, whereas the Hebrews were the working class, many were slaves, which provided the services and goods for the Egyptian way of life. Many skilled tradeswomen were used to make curtains, weave fabric, embroider and sew. The gold beaters and carvers who made the various Egyptian idols and statues with the work of their hands were exquisite.

The Hebrews were well trained in their trades and produced excellent work, as near enough was not good enough for their Egyptian employers, as only the best would have been acceptable. Making the chariot wheels and beating the iron, building the chariots and caring for the horses would necessitate stable hands, along with woodworkers, iron-mongers, and blacksmiths. These lists go on.

Building the Tabernacle

As the children of Israel were a nomadic tribe living in tents, a portable structure would suit their situation until they reached the Promised Land. Their past in Egypt had equipped the Israelites for the work involved in building and constructing a structure worthy of the presence of the Lord to dwell in. Moses called the people chosen by the Lord to carry out the necessary work of building, shaping, and weaving the various articles that would be used in their worship and feast days.

One could only imagine that the children of Israel would have been inquisitive as they saw the individual materials assembled and then placed side by side in a designated area, waiting for all to be completed. Not only men were given tasks, but skilled women in weaving, embroidery, curtain making, and garments for the priests to wear, along with many other trades, were called upon to offer only the best they could, and that was without blemish.

Construction of the Tabernacle and Various Items

Item	Reference	Construction	Reference
Offerings for the Sanctuary	Exodus 25:1–9	Materials given for the Tabernacle	Exodus 38:21–31
The Ark of the Testimony	Exodus 25:10–22	Making	Exodus 37:1–9
The Table of Shewbread	Exodus 25:23–30	Making	Exodus 37:10–16
The Gold Lampstand	Exodus 25:31–40	Making	Exodus 37:17–24
The Altar of Burnt Offering	Exodus 27:1–8	Making	Exodus 38:1–7
The Court of the Tabernacle	Exodus 27:9–19	Making	Exodus 38:9–20
The Care of the Lampstand	Exodus 27:20–21		
Garments for the Priesthood	Exodus 28:1–4	Making	Exodus 39:1
The Ephod	Exodus 28:5–14	Making	Exodus 39:2–7
The Breastplate	Exodus 28:15–30	Making	Exodus 39:8–21
Other Priestly Garments	Exodus 28:31–43	Making	Exodus 39:22–31
Aaron and his sons Consecrated	Exodus 29:1–37		
The Daily Offerings	Exodus 29:38–46		
The Altar of Incense	Exodus 30: 1–10	Making	Exodus 37:25–28
The Bronze Laver	Exodus 30:17–21	Making	Exodus 38:8
The Holy Anointing Oil	Exodus 30:22–33	Making	Exodus 37:29
The Incense	Exodus 30:34–38	Making	Exodus 37:29
The Tabernacle	Exodus 26:1–37	Finished	Exodus 39:43

The Tabernacle of the Lord

The day finally came when all the work was completed:

> *"Then Moses looked over all the work,*
> *and indeed they had done it;*
> *as the Lord had commanded,*
> *just so they had done it.*
> *And Moses blessed them."*
>
> Exodus 39:43

'Then the Lord spoke to Moses and instructed that on the first day of the first month you shall set up the Tabernacle of the tent of meeting'. Under the watchful eyes of Moses and the skilled trade people, the *'Tabernacle'* took shape. Slowly but surely, everything knit together in perfect harmony.

There were many components of the Tabernacle housed within the outer perimeter wall. Between the front gate and the Tabernacle Door, there was a Bronze Altar where the killed animal would be sacrificed. Directly behind the Bronze Altar was the Bronze Laver. This was for the priests to wash their hands and feet, and the mirrors embedded in the Laver would show whether their clothes were clean, as they could not enter the Tabernacle if they were unclean.

The Tabernacle had three curtains that protected the building from the elements. The inner curtain covered the walls and the roof area inside the Tabernacle. This curtain was adorned with cherubim, as were the curtains which formed a Door into the

Tabernacle and also separated the Holy Place from the Most Holy Place. The cherubim were perfectly woven on both sides, as this was the house of the Lord, the curtain separating the Holy Place and the Holy of Holies, no loose ends were left or seen.

Inside the Tabernacle, on the left-hand side, was the Candelabra. Three candles on either side of one central candle that was above the rest as all gave light to the interior. To the right was the Shewbread Table, where Presence Bread and Wine was placed, along with some utensils. The Altar of Incense provided a sweet-smelling savour to the atmosphere as the Altar represented the prayers made to Father God.

Directly behind the Altar was a curtain that separated the two areas, the 'Holy Place' and the 'Most Holy Place'. This curtain also had Cherubim embroidered into the fabric that was seen on both sides. The 'Ark of the Covenant' rested behind the curtain in the 'Holy of Holies', and only on one day of the year was a designated priest allowed to enter into this area.

"Then the cloud covered the Tabernacle of meeting,
and the glory of the Lord filled the Tabernacle.
For the cloud of the Lord
was above the Tabernacle by day, and fire was over it by night,
in the sight of all the house of Israel,
throughout all their journeys."

Exodus 40:34, 38

When the cloud began to move, Moses knew the time had arrived to pack and move camp, which meant dismantling the 'Tabernacle'. Only Levites, who were the appointed custodians of the Tabernacle, were allowed to carry out the sacrifices or touch the anointed articles or parts of the Tabernacle because the Tabernacle was Holy to the Lord.

Aaron and his sons had been consecrated to serve the Lord as His priests (Exodus 29:1–37), as strict instructions had been given regarding the Holy Anointing Oil (Exodus 30:22–33) and its use.

> *"With it you shall anoint the Tabernacle of meeting*
> *and the Ark of the Testimony;*
> *the table and all its utensils,*
> *and the lavar and its base.*
> *You shall consecrate them,*
> *that they may be most holy;*
> *whatever touches them must be holy."*
>
> Exodus 30:26–30

When the Lord chose to move camp, the Levites, who were the Lord's chosen priests, dismantled and re-assembled the Tabernacle. Aaron and his sons came and covered all the holy objects. Once this was completed, the sons of Kohath would carry the covered items but were forbidden to touch them. The sons of Gershon would carry the curtains and other parts associated with the curtains in the Tabernacle. The sons of Merari were assigned to carry the boards, bars, pillars, sockets and associated articles. Numbers 3:1 to 4:49

The Lord had instructed Moses to observe the 'Passover', so Moses carried out the instructions of the Lord. At the end of the celebrations, the cloud began to move. Everyone knew what this meant, as the Tabernacle was to be dismantled in the correct order by the designated people as each fulfilled his role. Had the people listened to the instructions given previously, and could they obey without question?

The Lord had given Moses instructions to make two 'Silver Trumpets' to be used by Aaron's sons, who were priests. These were to aid Moses when calling the congregation or the movement of the camp (Numbers 10:2). When both the trumpets were blown, the congregation would assemble, but if only one trumpet was blown, then the leaders and the heads of the divisions would assemble. When the advance was sounded, each tribe in order would begin their journey. Numbers 10:3–6

While most of the children of Israel packed their tents and belongings, the Levites were given an extra task as they were also required to pack and dismantle the 'Tabernacle'. One could imagine that the first time would be a little frustrating, as each waited for the previous group to finish their part before they could begin their task.

These operations were performed by the Levite families of Kohath, Gershom, and Merari under the control of Ithamar, the son of Aaron, the priest. On the day that the Tabernacle was set up, the leaders of Israel brought to Moses, as an offering to the Lord, six covered wagons and twelve oxen, and the Lord instructed Moses to accept them. Numbers 7:2–5

Two wagons with four oxen were given to the Gershonites, and four wagons with eight oxen to the Merarites. These wagons were to carry the items of the Tabernacle for which they were responsible, and these wagons were covered so that their contents were not exposed to the gaze of the Israelites. The Kohathites were given no wagons, as they had to bear the holy vessels *'upon their shoulders'*. Numbers 7:9

When all was ready, Moses would signal the sons of Aaron to blow the 'Advance' on the 'Silver Trumpets' as each tribe would file out in order as they followed the Priests bearing the 'Ark of the Testimony'. Everything was ordered by the Lord, which would avoid confusion:

> *"For God is not the author of confusion*
>
> *but of peace."*
>
> 1 Corinthians 14:33a

The Lord had given specific instructions to Moses about the order the tribes were to follow when the Israelites' camp was to move. First to lead the way were the eastern tribes of Judah, Issachar and Zebulun. The Tabernacle was then disassembled, and the Gershonites and the Merarites travelled behind the leading group carrying the Tabernacle. The southern tribes of

Reuben, Simeon, and Gad were followed by the Kohathites, who carried the holy things.

By the time the Kohathites arrived, the Tabernacle should have been erected so the holy things could be placed in their order, and then Aaron and his priests would uncover them away from the eyes of the children of Israel. The western tribes of Ephraim, Manasseh, and Benjamin were followed by the northern tribes of Dan, Asher, and Naphtali. Numbers 10:14–27.

```
          The Levites carried the covered
               Ark of the Covenant
               The Tribe of Judah
               The Tribe of Issachar
               The Tribe of Zebulun
The Levite Gershonite and Merarites with the oxen and carts
               The Tribe of Reuben
               The Tribe of Simeon
               The Tribe of Gad
    The Levite Kohathites carried the covered Holy Things
               The Tribe of Ephraim
               The Tribe of Manasseh
               The Tribe of Benjamin
               The Tribe of Dan
               The Tribe of Asher
               The Tribe of Naphatali
```

When the people departed from Horeb (Mt Sinai) and commenced their journey, there was one matter that could not be overlooked. The Ark was not to be found amid the people behind the second group, in front of the tribe of Ephraim, as had been instructed. The Psalmist later wrote:

> *"Give ear, O Shepherd of Israel,*
> *You who lead Joseph like a flock;*
> *You who dwell between the cherubim,*
> *shine forth!*
> *Before Ephraim, Benjamin, and Manasseh,*
> *stir up your strength,*
> *and come and save us."*
>
> Psalm 80:2–3

There was a change in the order of the march, and the Ark was out in front leading the way, so what caused this change? It was due to the request that Moses made to his brother-in-law Hobab that he should accompany them and guide them through the wilderness, showing them where to camp, as he could be their eyes (Numbers 10:32). In grace, but also as a rebuke to Moses, the order of the march was altered so that the Ark was out in front.

> *"So they departed from the mountain of the Lord*
> *on a journey of three days;*
> *and the Ark of the Covenant of the Lord*
> *went before them for the three days' journey,*
> *to search out a resting place for them."*
>
> Numbers 10:33

The priests bearing the 'Ark of Testimony' led a three-day journey until the cloud paused, as the children of Israel came to Kibroth Hattaavah, where the Tabernacle was set up in the reverse order of the dismantling. When the Tabernacle was reconstructed in compliance with the instructions of the Lord, the cloud descended and covered the Tabernacle. Numbers 10:36

The Lord moved the Tabernacle from Kibroth Hattaavah to Hazeroth and then onto Rithmah in the Wilderness of Paran. The Lord again spoke to Moses and told him to send out twelve leaders, one from each of the tribes, to spy out the land of Canaan. Moses did as he was commanded and sent them out. After forty days, the selected leaders returned and brought their reports.

Ten of the leaders refused to trust the Lord, as they brought bad reports of the land, saying that the Israelites would not defeat the giants in the land of Canaan. Although the Lord had delivered them from Egypt and provided for their needs, these leaders refused to trust the Lord and turned the children of Israel against Moses. Only two faithful leaders, Joshua and Caleb, brought good reports.

Because ten doubted the power of the Lord to deliver their enemies into their hands, the Lord brought punishment on all those who were twenty years and older and were never to enter the land of promise. Joshua and Caleb were the exception because they believed and trusted the Lord to provide.

The Children of Israel now faced death in the desert, as they would wander aimlessly for forty years. Only those under twenty years of age would inherit the promises promised to Abraham. They had set up and dismantled the Tabernacle three times, another thirty times would be their privilege before they reached Acacia Grove in the plains of Moab, directly across from the city of Jericho on the Jordan River.

Wilderness of Sinai. Mount Sinai	Jotbathah
Kibroth Hattaavah	Abronah
Hazeroth	Ezion Geber
Rithmah	Wilderness of Zin, which is Kadesh
Spies sent out. Wilderness Journey begins	Mount Hor
Rimmon Perez	Zalmonah
Libnah	Punon
Rissah	Oboth
Kehelathah	Ije Abarim
Mount Shepher	Dibon Gad
Haradah	Almon Diblathaim
Makheloth	Mountains of Abarim
Tahath	Abel Acacia Grove in the plains of Moab
Terah	Crossed Jordan River
Mithkah	Gilgal
Hashmonah	Shiloh
Moseroth	Nob
Bene Jaakan	Gibeon
Hor Hagidgad	Solomon's Temple

Thoughts to Ponder

Moses said to Hobob, his brother-in-law, "You be our eyes." Moses, the leader, was open to wrong thinking and decisions, just as the people he was sent to lead. Moses was saying, "While the Lord has led us this far, I want you to take His place as I trust you to find us the right place to camp."

This was never going to happen, and the Lord graciously corrected Moses of his wrong thinking. When the march proceeded, the covered Ark of the Covenant was leading the way, not with the other covered articles. The Ark of the Covenant was showing the way, as Hobob was not directing the proceedings.

> *"A man's heart plans his way,*
> *but the Lord directs his steps."*
>
> Proverbs 16:9

We should not be too critical of Moses, as our actions may have been no different from what his were. How often do we fail in the matter of guidance? It may be because we fail to hear the sound of the silver trumpet and give a correct response to the sound.

> *"He who has an ear,*
> *let him hear what the Spirit*
> *says to the churches."*
>
> Revelation 2:29, 3:6, 13

When the cloud moved and began to rise, the priests and Levites, those who lived nearest to the Sanctuary, would be the first to understand it was time to break camp and move. So it is that those who live closest to the Lord should be more able to discern the mind of the Lord and His thoughts for each of us.

> *"Whenever the cloud was taken up*
> *from above the Tabernacle,*
> *after that the children of Israel would journey."*
>
> Numbers 9:17

The lesson for us to learn is that as we journey through life, we should be careful to move only when we are directed. With decisions aligning with the known will of the Lord, we need to follow His direction, as we must always be careful to seek the thoughts and guidance of the Lord on our journey together.

> *"But to sons of Kohath*
> *he (Moses) gave none,*
> *because theirs was the service of the holy things,*
> *which they carried on their shoulders."*
>
> Numbers 7:9

The Korahites Levite priests carried the covered holy articles on their shoulders. Each one of the holy articles housed in the Holy Place represented a part of God's Holy Law, just as the Ark of the Testament, which rested in the Holy of Holies, contained the Law and other reminders of the Law, so the priests carried the articles on their shoulders.

Just as the priests bore the Tabernacle articles on their shoulders, so Jesus bore the crossbeam on His shoulders as the weight of the Law was upon Him. Just as the Priests were obedient to the known will of Father God, so was Jesus, who became our Great High Priest, who carried our sin on His shoulders, and became the perfect sacrifice for us all.

What is a lesson we can apply to ourselves concerning the moving of the camp? The Levite priests were allotted specific duties to perform, but no one tried to do someone else's job. Those who wrapped didn't carry, just as those who dismantled didn't carry the Ark of the Covenant.

In the body of Christ, there are many parts (1 Corinthians 12:12–27). We all have our part to play and should not go outside what Father God has instructed us to do. Some are called to visitation, whereas others are called to teach. Some are called to manage finances, and others are called to organise. We should never try to do what Father God has not equipped us to carry out.

> *"For God is not the author of confusion but of peace."*
>
> 1 Corinthians 14:33a

The Tabernacle's Journey in the Promised Land

The Tabernacle was made at Mount Sinai in the year after the Exodus and continued until the fourth year of King Solomon, nearly five hundred years later, when the Temple superseded the Tabernacle in Jerusalem. During that five hundred years, virtually all that is known about the Tabernacle has to be pieced together from occasional references in scripture and isolated texts.

The Tabernacle was a transportable building consisting of two apartments, the 'Holy Place' and the 'Most Holy Place', surrounded by a 'Court' bound by curtains on poles about seven feet high. Within its boundaries, the central worship of Israel was conducted, the solemn ceremonies of sacrifice and cleansing, including the all-important annual 'Day of Atonement', which ritually cleansed Israel from sin.

The Lord was pictured as dwelling within the 'Most Holy Place', forever hidden from sight. Only the High Priest could enter that sacred apartment when, once a year, he went in to make atonement for the people. Wherever the people went, the Tabernacle went with them, taken down and re-erected every time they moved a stage further in their journey.

The unknown history of the Tabernacle commenced when their forty years of wilderness wanderings were over, and the Israelites crossed the Jordan River into the Promised Land. Their first thought was to re-erect the Tabernacle in what they hoped would be its permanent location, although that hope was not to be fulfilled. A site was found near Jericho, a level uninhabited plain, and here, the limits of Israel's camp in their designated areas with the Tabernacle erected in the centre. They named the place Gilgal, meaning a great circle. Joshua 4:19–20

The Tabernacle remained at Gilgal for about seven years whilst the Israelite warriors were conquering the land. It soon became apparent that Gilgal was not a good choice. A central location was needed, somewhere in the natural centre of the land. A place was found between Dan in the north and Beersheba in the south, Gilgal in the east and Joppa in the west. A complete circle of hills created a plain about ten miles across, in the centre of which was a slightly elevated area.

They named the place Shiloh, and here, the entire nation gathered to see the Tabernacle erected and to make this their national place of meeting (Joshua 18:1). It was here that the will of the Lord concerning tribal territories was sought by the casting of lots. The Tabernacle remained at Shiloh for about three hundred and fifty years until the disastrous time of Eli, the High Priest in the days of Samuel.

As the years passed by, a settlement of priests and Levites attended to the sanctuary's needs, which developed into a sizable town. It could have been a holy town, a place memorable for the devotion of its inhabitants to Israel's God. Unfortunately, it became the reverse until the Lord allowed Shiloh to be destroyed by the enemies of Israel and never inhabited again.

Only a few years after the death of Joshua, while Phinehas, the grandson of Aaron, was still High Priest, as they did not do what was right in the sight of the Lord, a scandalous decision showed how quickly and how far Israel had fallen from the high ideals of their covenant with the Lord.

A certain Levite of Mount Ephraim, a few miles from Shiloh, was passing through Gibeah of Benjamin with his concubine and had her seized, maltreated and killed by some unruly Benjamites. The outcome was against the people of Gibeah, which developed into a war of revenge by all the other tribes against Benjamin. Judges 19:1 to 20:48

The consequence was that almost the entire tribe of Benjamin were wiped out except for about six hundred men. The victors then came to the Tabernacle and complained to the Lord that a tribe had been lost out of Israel, as the other tribes had sworn before the Lord that none of them would ever give their daughters in marriage to a Benjamite. In this extremity, the elders of Israel developed a plan to overcome the difficulty. Judges 21:17–24

There was to be a feast at Shiloh in which the 'daughters of Shiloh' came out and danced. The men of Benjamin were to lie in wait, abduct the girls and retreat to their hometown, and nothing would be done by their enemies in war.

Not made apparent in the story is the fact that these *'daughters of Shiloh'* were the young virgin daughters of the priests who attended to their duties in the Tabernacle. The young girls' lives were consecrated and devoted to sacred services, as dancing was an expression of their worship, which was enjoyed at the Feast of Tabernacles, the only feast that encouraged dancing.

The fact that the elders of Israel should recommend and the priests in charge sanction so gross a contempt of the Tabernacle service and worship is a measure of the extent to which, in less than a couple of generations, Israel had fallen short of its high ideals. One could say that the glory of the Tabernacle began to depart almost as soon as it was erected at Shiloh.

For more than two hundred years after this, the story of the Tabernacle is a blank; nothing is known of its history. This is the period of the oppression of Israel by the Moabites, the Syrians and the Philistines, which in itself indicates that Israel had largely turned away from God, and so earned the penalty of the violated Covenant. It is of this period that the writer of Judges says:

> *'In those days there was no king in Israel;*
> *every man did that which was right in his own eyes."*

Judges 21:25

It was a time of anarchy in which a few remained faithful to Israel's God, and the rest were indifferent. Towards the end of this period came the upheaval in the Priesthood, which resulted in the line of Eleazar being deposed and priests of the line of Ithamar, Aaron's younger son, seizing the duties of office.

Eli, of the line of Ithamar, was serving as High Priest when he noticed a woman kneeling at the gate of the Tabernacle. The priest, thinking she was drunk, rebuked her. Elkanah and Hanna were from the tribe of the Levites (1 Chronicles 6:33–34). Once Hannah explained she was praying, the priest blessed her and asked God to grant her request. She returned home and was able to conceive, then bore a son whom they named 'Samuel', which means, *"Because I have asked for him from the Lord."* 1 Samuel 1:20

Once Samuel was weaned, Hannah and Samuel travelled to Shiloh, taking a sacrifice with them. After the sacrifice is offered, Hannah presents the young Samuel to Eli and says, *"For this child I prayed, and the Lord has granted me my petition which I asked of Him. Therefore I also have lent him to the Lord."* 1 Samuel 1:27–28a

It is then revealed that Eli's sons were wicked men who did evil in the Tabernacle (1 Chronicles 2:12–17, 22–25), in contrast:

"But Samuel ministered before the Lord,

even as a child,

wearing a linen ephod."

1 Samuel 2:18

Hannah was able to see Samuel, who was in the care of the high priest Eli, at least once a year when she and her husband went up to offer the annual sacrifice, Hannah would always take along a little robe for Samuel. And *"Eli would bless Elkanah and his wife, saying, 'May the Lord give you descendants from this woman for the loan that was given to the Lord'."* 1 Samuel 2:20

Samuel would go on to become the spiritual leader of Israel, as the prophet and judge of the nation, Samuel would anoint the nation's first two kings, Saul and David.

About twenty years later came a great tragedy, as the warriors of Israel, beaten in conflict with their long-standing enemies, the Philistines, decided to take the sacred symbol of the Divine presence with them, the 'Ark of the Covenant', into battle. From its place in the 'Most Holy Place' of the Tabernacle, they carried it into battle before them, in the belief that God would never allow it to fall into the hands of the uncircumcised, and so victory would be assured.

This act of sacrilege met with due retribution, as the Lord allowed the sacred 'Ark' to fall into the hands of the Philistines and the Israelites were soundly defeated for a second time. The High Priest Eli, when news that the 'Ark of the Covenant' had been captured was brought to him, fell off his seat, broke his neck and died.

This was not only the end of Shiloh, but it also marked a turning point in the Lord's dealings with Israel. At first, Joseph had received the birthright from his father, Jacob, who passed it on to his son Ephraim. Now, the tribe of Ephraim, in whose territory Shiloh stood, had become the leading idolatrous tribe in Israel. This supreme example of their godlessness moved the Lord to reject Ephraim and pass the birthright to Judah, as represented in his descendant David, soon to be born.

Selected verses from Psalm 78 record the sad circumstances of that fatal battle, the loss of the 'Ark' and the Lord's consequent action:

"The children of Ephraim, being armed and carrying bows, turned back in the day of battle. They kept not the covenant of God and refused to walk in his law…they provoked him to anger with their high places, and moved him to jealousy with their graven images. When God heard this he was wroth, and greatly abhorred Israel, so that he forsook the tabernacle of Shiloh, the tent which he placed among men; and delivered his strength into captivity and his glory into the enemy's hand … the fire consumed their young men; their priests fell by the sword… he refused the tabernacle of Joseph, and chose not the tribe of Ephraim, but chose the tribe of Judah, the Mount Zion which he loved." Psalm 78: 9–70

It was at this point that Judah became the royal tribe of Israel, destined to produce Israel's kings.

The Old Testament gives no hint of what happened to the priestly settlement surrounding the Tabernacle. One could imagine that the Philistines, flushed with victory and capture of the 'Ark', soon covered the forty miles from Beth-Shemesh, where the battle was fought and demolished the little town. Shiloh was erased from the face of the earth.

Five hundred years later, the Lord said to Israel through the prophet Jeremiah, reproving them for their apostasy:

"But go now to My place which was in Shiloh,
where I set My name at the first,
and see what I did to it
because of the wickedness of My people Israel."
"Therefore I will do to the house
(Temple at Jerusalem)
which is called by My name,
in which you trust,
and to this place which I gave to you and your fathers,
as I have done to Shiloh."

Jeremiah 7:12, 14

It is probable that before the Philistines had reached Shiloh, Samuel, and the other Priests with him, succeeded in dismantling the Tabernacle and transported it out of harm's way. With the death of Eli, Samuel remained the only person of authority in Israel, and he probably assumed control. He re-erected the Tabernacle on its original site at Gilgal, without the Ark of the Covenant, and there it remained for something like fifty years into the reign of Saul.

It was at Gilgal that Samuel offered the sacrifices connected with Saul's appointment as king and at Gilgal that Saul was formally crowned king over Israel (I Samuel 10:8, 11:15). The High Priesthood was restored to the legal line of Eleazar in the person of Ahitub, father of the Zadok of David's time. Because in the absence of the 'Ark', the 'Day of Atonement' ritual could not be performed, Ahitub was merely given the courtesy title of *"Ruler of the House of God."* 1 Chronicles 9:15; Nehemiah 11:11

Saul became king, but after he disagreed with Samuel (1 Samuel 13:11–14), he took matters into his own hands, dismissed Ahitub and moved the Tabernacle to Nob, on the north side of Jerusalem. He appointed as High Priest Ahimelech, son of another Ahitub, a grandson of Eli, who, as a child, had survived the massacre at Shiloh. 1 Samuel 14:3

This arrangement did not last long, as Saul, suspecting Ahimelech of treasonable communication with David, sent men and massacred the entire priesthood of Nod. Abiathar, son of Ahimelech, alone escaping, removed the Tabernacle to his hometown of Gibeon (1 Samuel 22:9–23). This fact is known only by inference.

When, later on, David became king of all Israel, the Tabernacle, complete with the altar of burnt offering but without the 'Ark', was standing at Gibeon. Zadok, of the line of Eleazar, was its priest (1 Chronicles 16:39, 21:29). This must have been done by Saul after his slaughter of the priesthood at Nob. Here, it stood throughout the reign of David and until Solomon became the new leader of Israel. 1 Kings 3:4, 2 Chronicles 1:3–15

Saul had died, and David was king over all of Israel. Somewhere about the twelfth year of his reign, he decided to bring the 'Ark of the Covenant', which had laid in the house of Abinadab in Judah for about seventy years. As this attempt failed, three months later, David went to the house of Obed-Edom and brought the Ark of the Covenant to Jerusalem. He erected what was a replica of the Tabernacle 'Most Holy Place' and 'Holy Place', with an altar for offerings, and eventually installed the 'Ark' in its proper place, to the rejoicing of all Israel.

He did not, however, interfere with the true Tabernacle, with its Brazen Altar made by Moses, at Gibeon. Thus, for another thirty years, there were two Tabernacles in Israel and two High Priests. The original Tabernacle was at Gibeon with Zadok of the legal line of Eleazar, the third son of Aaron, serving as the High Priest, but the Levitical sacrifices could not be performed there because it did not possess the 'Ark of the Covenant'.

The new Tabernacle at Jerusalem had the 'Ark' and a new altar for burnt offerings, but the High Priest was Abiathar of the condemned line of Ithamar, the fourth son of Aaron. At neither place could the full ceremonies demanded by the Law be carried out, and it is probable that the annual 'Day of Atonement' sacrifice had long since become obsolete.

Solomon had spent time at the Gibeon Tabernacle, as this was where the Lord appeared to Him in a dream by night and said, *"Ask! What shall I give you?"* (1 Kings 3:5). Solomon saw the significance in the old Tabernacle which his father had missed. So, he reunited the Holy Articles from both Tabernacles.

> *"Then they brought up the Ark of the Lord,*
> *the Tabernacle of meeting,*
> *and all the holy furnishings*
> *that were in the Tabernacle."*
>
> 1 Kings 8:4

It was left to Solomon to regularise this state of affairs. As soon as the Temple was completed and dedicated in the fourth year of his reign, he had the 'Ark of the Covenant' brought into Solomen's Temple (2 Chronicles 5:5) and instituted a grand opening ceremony. Zadok was appointed High Priest, thus fulfilling the condemnation passed upon Eli (1 Samuel 2:29–32) and his posterity a century earlier.

The meeting place between God and men, made by Bezaleel under Moses' direction at the time of the Exodus, came to its end. It had been the centre of Israel's worship for about five hundred years and now gave place to a greater and more permanent Temple.

Part 3

The Journey of the Ark of the Covenant

The Ark of the Covenant

"Then the temple of God was opened in heaven,
and the ark of His covenant was seen in His temple.
And there were lightnings,
noises, thunderings,
an earthquake, and great hail."

Revelation 11:19

As the most tangible symbol of the Lord's presence among the Israelites, the 'Ark of the Covenant' played the central role in the worship and religious life of Israel until it was lost or destroyed during the Babylonian destruction of Jerusalem in 586 B.C. 2 Kings 25:1–21; 2 Chronicles 36:17–21; Jerimiah 39:1–10; 52:1–30

The 'Ark of Testimony' was the first to be designed, fashioned and consecrated at Mount Sinai, then carried covered to each destination, including the Israelites' wilderness travels. The very construction of the Ark, an ornamented box fitted with poles to be transported from place to place, signifies the nomadic life of the early Israelites, as does the construction of the Tabernacle, the portable worship structure in which the Ark of the Covenant was housed.

The Lord's first recorded conversation spoken to Moses was at the unconsumed burning bush in the back of the desert near Mount Sinai. Moses had an ordained journey to complete over the next forty years that would bring him back to Mount Sinai, where the Lord would reveal intimate details for the implementation of a new relationship with Him, a new way of living, and an understanding of the One who provides for His chosen people, the children of Israel.

Moses returned to Egypt, and after the plagues, the crossing of the Red Sea, and the encampment at Mount Sinai were all completed, Moses was instructed to build a Tabernacle for the presence of the Lord to dwell in. The 'Ark of the Covenant', or 'Testimony', was the first piece of furniture to be made, as nothing else was more important or came before Father God.

> *"You shall make a mercy seat of pure gold;*
> *and you shall make two cherubim of gold;*
> *of hammered work you shall make them at*
> *the two ends of the mercy seat.*
> *And the cherubim shall stretch out their wings above,*
> *covering the mercy seat with their wings,*

and they shall face one another;

the faces of the cherubim shall be toward the mercy seat."

Exodus 25:10–20 (selected)

Once the Tabernacle and all the furnishings had been completed and consecrated, the glory of the Lord descended and filled the Tabernacle. It is to be expected that when Moses, a Levite, went into the Tabernacle, the Lord would speak to him and outline any further plans He had for the Israelites.

"Now when Moses went into the

Tabernacle of Meeting to speak with Him,

he heard the voice of One speaking to him

from above the mercy seat

that was on the Ark of testimony,

from between the two cherubim;

thus He spoke to him."

Numbers 7:89

Only the selected priest, once a year, could enter the 'Holy of Holies' where the 'Ark of the Covenant' was located. Just as the way to the *Tree of Life* was guarded by cherubim, so too was the mercy seat, as their wings protected the way to Father God and the Mercy Seat. Their faces focused on the Mercy Seat as they looked to the day when the way would once again be opened to fellowship with Father God.

Inside the 'Ark of Testimony' were the two tablets on which were written the agreement or covenant the Lord had made with the Israelites. Aaron's Rod was a reminder that God does not put up with rebellion against Himself or His chosen representatives on earth, as his rod remained in the 'Ark of the Covenant' as a testimony of God's choice of Aaron and Moses to lead His people.

The Lord had also told Moses to collect an omer of manna and place it in the *'Ark of Testimony'*.

> *Moses said to Aaron,*
> *"Take a pot and put an omer of manna in it,*
> *and lay it up before the Lord,*
> *to be kept for your generations."*
>
> Exodus 16:33

When the cloud moved, this signalled that the camp was to move to a new destination, which meant the Tabernacle was required to be dismantled as the priests followed the procedure the Lord had provided for Moses to observe. After Aaron and his sons had covered the holy things, the duty of the Kohathites was to carry them. The dismantling of the Tabernacle was the responsibility of the sons of Gershon and the sons of Merari.

While the cloud led the way, the priests bearing the *'Ark of the Covenant'* on their shoulders would lead the tribes (Numbers

10:33). The tribes of Judah, Issachar and Zebulun followed, then the sons of Gershon and the sons of Merari, as they drove the oxen and wagons which contained the Tabernacle structure. The tribes of Reuben, Simeon and Gad followed as the Kohathites carried the covered holy things, and then the tribes of Ephram, Benjamin, and Manasseh were followed by the tribes of Dan, Asher and Naphtali.

The Tabernacle would be dismantled and reassembled thirty times over the next forty-plus years until they reached Acacia Grove in the plains of Moab, where the Tabernacle was set up at the Jordan River across from the city of Jericho.

When the camp moved, the cloud went before, as the Priests carrying the 'Ark of the Covenant' followed, each of their steps walked a predestined path. As you meditate on the scene that has been drawn, the cloud is represented by the Holy Spirit. The 'Ark of the Covenant' represented Father God, while the steps of the priests were guided by the Lord or Jesus. So we have a Trinity, three separate, but all three working together as One.

Many lessons were learnt regarding the handling of the 'Ark of the Covenant' and the offerings which could or could not be used. One such time was when Aaron's eldest son Nadab and his brother Abihu, both Levite priests, chose to offer profane fire to the Lord. A conflict may have existed within the priesthood between a group led by Nadab and Abihu and a group of priests who remained faithful to the sacred worship led by Mishael and Elzaphan.

Nadab and his brother Abihu offered profane fire before the Lord, which He had not commanded them to do, so the fire went out from the Lord and devoured them, and they died before the Lord. The nature of their offence was to offer profane fire, which appears to refer to idolatrous worship. They had taken fire for their censers from a place other than the altar fire, which was the only legitimate fire for the worship. Leviticus 10:1–7

The children of Israel had travelled from Kadesh to Mount Hor. The care of the 'Ark of the Covenant', the holy things, along with the supervision of the sacrifices and services, was about to change. The Lord revealed to Moses that Aaron was to be *'gathered to his people'*, so a new priest was chosen by the Lord to replace Aaron, and the Lord chose Eleazar, Aaron's third son. Moses, Aaron and Eleazar climbed Mount Hor, where the priestly robes of Aaron were placed on his son, and Aaron joined his ancestors. Numbers 20:22–26

The camp at Acacia Grove was on the move as Eleazar and the other priests covered the holy things ready for transport. Joshua commanded the priests to take up the 'Ark of the Covenant' and cross over before the people.

"When you have come to the edge
of the water of the Jordan,
you shall stand in the Jordan.
As soon as the souls of the feet of the priests

rest in the waters of the Jordan,

the waters shall be cut off."

Joshua 3:8–13 selected

"While the priests who bore the Ark of the Covenant of the Lord stood firm on dry ground in the midst of the Jordan, all Israel crossed over on dry ground, until all the people had crossed completely over the Jordan." Joshua 3:17

"Then it came to pass, when all the people had completely crossed over, that the Ark of the Lord and the priests crossed over in the presence of the people." Joshua 4:11

The 'Ark of the Covenant' was placed in the 'Holy of Holies' in the Tabernacle situated at Gilgal. After some days had passed, the priests covered the 'Ark of the Covenant', but none of the other holy things. As they left the holy place, seven priests who had ram's horn trumpets formed up and marched in front of the covered 'Ark of the Covenant'.

The march was different to anything that had happened in the past. The armed men went before the priests who blew the ram's horns, followed by the priests bearing the 'Ark of the Covenant', and the rear guard came after the Ark while the priests continued blowing the trumpets. Apart from the ram's horns, nothing else could be heard. After they had gone around the city of Jericho once, they all returned to camp, and the 'Ark of the Covenant' was placed back in the 'Holy of Holies' and uncovered.

This procedure was carried out for six days, exactly as the first, but then it changed. On the seventh day, the procession marched around six times, each time exactly the same as the preceding six days, but the seventh time was different. Apart from the priests with ram's horns, two priests were carrying the silver trumpets, which did not accompany the marchers on the other days.

Moses had told the people to shout when they heard the sound of the trumpets. As they came to the end of the sixth time around and began the seventh, Joshua signalled the priests who had the silver trumpets to sound the advance, and when they did, all the people shouted with a great shout, and the wall fell down flat. Joshua 6:1–20a

The priests bearing the 'Ark of the Covenant' walked back to the camp at Gilgal and placed the 'Ark of the Covenant' in the 'Holy of Holies', where it was uncovered and rested in its place.

About seven years had passed when the priests covered all the holy things, and the 'Ark of the Covenant' led the way to Shiloh, where the Tabernacle had been set up, and once again, the Ark was placed in the 'Holy of Holies', as the congregation observed all the laws and ordinances written in the Law, given by Father God to Moses on Mount Sinai.

For about three hundred and fifty years, the Tabernacle that contained the 'Ark of the Covenant' rested at Shiloh. Joshua, their leader and Eleazer, the priest, had died, and many other priests had attended to the Tabernacle requirements. Eli, the high priest, was a descendant of Ithamar, the fourth son of Arron, not Eleazer, the third son, who was responsible for the Tabernacle along with his two sons, Hophni and Phinehas, but both the sons did evil in the sight of the Lord.

A young boy by the name of Samuel was brought by his parents, Elkanah and Hanna, who were from the tribe of the Levites but lived in Ephraim, brought Samuel to serve in the Tabernacle with Eli, devoted wholly to the Lord. The following is written about Samuel:

> *"But Samuel ministered before the Lord,*
>
> *even as a child,*
>
> *wearing a linen ephod"*

1 Samuel 2:18

The Israelites looked to the past and did not ask the Lord what they should do but instead applied their own wisdom to combat a situation. They had forgotten the 'Ark of the Covenant' was the seat of the Lord in His Temple in the Tabernacle. To remove the Ark would mean removing His divine protection and incurring His wrath, which meant when they removed the Ark, it would be like throwing their weapons over the walls.

The priests, under the direction of Hophni and Phinehas, covered the 'Ark of the Covenant' but none of the other holy things. The Ark was carried to Beth-Shemesh or Ebenezer, where the Israelites waged a second war against the Philistines, where four thousand Israelites were killed along with Hophni and

Phinehas. The 'Ark of the Covenant' was now in the possession of the Philistines, who brought the 'Ark of the Covenant' into the house of Dagon and set it by Dagon, which was situated at Ashdod. 1 Samuel 5:1–2

The presence of the 'Ark of the Covenant' was released upon these unsuspecting Philistines.

> *"When the people of Ashdod*
> *arose early in the morning, there was Dagon,*
> *fallen on its face to the earth before the Lord.*
> *So they took Dagon and set it in its place again."*
>
> 1 Samuel 5:3

But the drama had only just begun:

> *"When they arose early the next morning,*
> *there was Dagon, fallen on its face to the ground*
> *before the Ark of the Lord.*
> *The head of Dagon and both the palms of its hands*
> *were broken off on the threshold;*
> *only Dagon's torso was left of it."*
>
> 1 Samuel 5:4

The Ark of the Covenant

The tribe of Dan had inherited the land of the Philistines many years previous but had failed to change the people and their worship to the One True God of the Israelites. As the Philistines worshipped Dagon, they were unaware that the Lord, who accompanied the 'Ark of the Covenant', had laws to be obeyed. They had broken at least four of the commandments.

- *You shall have no other gods before Me.*
- *You shall not make idols.*
- *You shall not steal.*
- *You shall not covert.*

The Lord had dethroned their god; now, the people bore His wrath as He attacked their bodies and health, as the Lord caused tumours to form on the Philistines who were in Ashdod and its territory. The tumours caused swollen lymph glands, symptoms that accompanied some form of bubonic plague carried by rats.

The 'Ark of the Covenant' was then sent to the city of Gath, but the hand of the Lord was against the city with great destruction as He struck the men of the city, both small and great, with tumours. The 'Ark of the Covenant' was sent to another city, Ekron, but the Ekronites cried out, saying:

> *"They have brought the Ark of the God of Israel to us,
> to kill us and our people!"*
>
> 1 Samuel 5:10b

All the lords of the Philistines unanimously agreed to send the ark of God of Israel back to its own place, for there was deadly destruction throughout the city, as the hand of God was very heavy there.

> *"And the men who did not die*
> *were stricken with tumours,*
> *and the cry of the city went up to heaven."*
>
> 1 Samuel 5:12

The presence of the 'Ark of the Covenant' certainly impacted the Philistines, as no prayer was made to Dagon but to Father God, the God of the Israelites.

Seven months had passed since the battle of the Israelites and the Philistines. The Philistines inquired of their priests and diviners as to what course of action they were to take. They replied:

> *"If you send away the ark of the God of Israel,*
> *do not send it empty; but by all means*
> *return it to Him with a trespass offering."*
>
> 1 Samuel 6:3a

A trespass offering is the final Levitical sacrifice required of the Israelites. Although it is similar to the sin offering (Leviticus 7:7), there are several differences. The sin offering deals with sin against God; the trespass offering emphasises sin against God and man. At least one Philistine priest understood the Covenant Law given to them so many years previous. The Philistines were returning the 'Ark of the Covenant' to God (Him), as well as the Israelites.

A new cart was made and hitched to two milk cows that had never been yoked, the 'Ark of the Covenant' was then placed in the new cart, along with a trespass offering of five gold rats and five gold tumours, all in a box of their own, placed next to the 'Ark of the Covenant'. 1 Samuel 6:3–11

> *"Then the cows headed straight*
> *for the road to Beth Shemesh,*
> *and went along the highway,*
> *lowing as they went,*
> *and did not turn aside to the*
> *right hand or the left."*
>
> 1 Samuel 6:12

The cart stopped in the field of Joshua of Beth Shemesh, where some of the men looked inside the 'Ark of the Covenant', and because they violated a consecrated vessel, the Lord inflicted the same plague on seventy of them, then fifty thousand in the same area. The men of Beth Shemesh sent messengers to the inhabitants of Kirjath Jearim to come and take the 'Ark of the Covenant' away.

> *"Then the men of Kirjath Jearim*
> *came and took the Ark of the Lord,*
> *and brought it into the house of*
> *Abinadab on the hill,*
> *and consecrated Eleaser his son*
> *to keep the Ark of the Lord."*
>
> 1 Samuel 7:1

Seventy years were to pass before the priests arrived at the house of Abinadab, King Saul's son, covered the ark and placed it on a new cart, which was hitched to some oxen. Uzzah and Ahio, the sons of Abinadab, the grandsons of Saul, were part of the procession as Ahio went before the cart leading the oxen, and Uzzah stood nearby. When the procession came to Nachon's threshing floor, the oxen stumbled, so Uzzah put out his hand to steady the 'Ark of the Covenant' but was struck dead immediately. 2 Samuel 6:6

Because David and the people did not understand why this had occurred, the 'Ark of the Covenant' was taken to the house of Obed-Edom the Gittite. While the 'Ark of the Covenant' was in the home of Obed-Edom, the Lord blessed him, all his household, and all that belonged to him. 2 Samuel 6:11–12

Three months had passed, and the priests arrived and covered the 'Ark of the Covenant' as it was about to continue its journey. Instead of the covered 'Ark of the Covenant' being placed in a cart drawn by oxen, the priest bore the covered 'Ark of the Covenant' on their shoulders to Jerusalem, where David placed the 'Ark of the Covenant' in a special Tabernacle (2 Samuel 6:17) built by David for the 'Ark of the Covenant' to rest.

The question could be asked, "Why David wanted the 'Ark of the Covenant' in his Tabernacle in Jerusalem?" David wanted to bring the 'Ark of the Covenant' to his capital city, Jerusalem, because he believed that the Ark was a powerful symbol of God's presence and would bring the people closer to the Lord.

David should have taken the 'Ark of the Covenant' to Gibeon, where the original Tabernacle stood, not to Jerusalem, where David had erected a replica Tabernacle. How could the Lord trust David to build the Temple when he had built a replica of the Tabernacle? There should have only been one Tabernacle for the 'Ark of the Covenant' to be placed in.

Zadok arrived at the Tabernacle, where he joined Abiathar and wrapped the 'Ark of the Covenant'. The priests carried the 'Ark of the Covenant' and crossed the Kidron Brook to where David was standing. Then David said to Zadok, the priest:

> *"Carry the Ark of God back into the city.*
> *If I find favour in the eyes of the Lord,*
> *He will bring me back and show me*
> *both it and His dwelling place."*
>
> 2 Samuel 15:25

The Journey of the Ark of Testimony in 1–2 Samuel

Scripture	Comment
1 Samuel 3:3	The Lord calls to Samuel sleeping in the tent of meeting, "where the Ark of God was."
1 Samuel 4	Philistines capture the Ark (for seven months: 1 Sam. 6:1)
1 Samuel 5:1–7	Philistines bring the Ark to Ashdod, setting it up next to the idol Dagon
1 Samuel 5:8–9	Philistines bring the Ark to Gath
1 Samuel 5:10–12	Philistines send the Ark to Ekron
1 Samuel 6:10–15	Philistines return the Ark with guilt offering to Beth-shemesh
1 Samuel 6:19–21	The Lord strikes 70 men for looking into the Ark
1 Samuel 7:1–2	Men of Kiriath-jearim take the Ark to the house of Abinadab (where it stays for 20 years)
1 Samuel 14:18	Saul commands Ahijah to bring the Ark to the war camp
2 Samuel 6:2–5	David begins to move the Ark to Jerusalem on a cart
2 Samuel 6:6–7	The Lord strikes Uzzah dead for holding on to the Ark
2 Samuel 6:10–11	David takes the Ark to the house of Obed-edom, where it stays for three months
2 Samuel 6:12–17	David brings the Ark to Jerusalem, and places it inside the tent he pitched for it
2 Samuel 15:24–25	Zadok brings the Ark to David, who commands him to carry it back to Jerusalem
2 Samuel 15:29	Zadok and Abiathar carry the Ark back to Jerusalem

The 'Ark of the Covenant' was uncovered when it was at rest in the 'Holy of Holies' in David's makeshift Tabernacle. About thirty years would pass before the 'Ark of the Covenant' would make its final journey from the Tabernacle built by David to Solomon's Temple (1 Kings 8:4, 2 Chronicles 5:5), where it would remain for about four hundred years when Nebuchadnezzar in 597 BC attacked Jerusalem and plundered the Temple.

> *"And he carried out from there*
> *all the treasures of the house of the Lord*
> *and the treasures of the king's house,*
> *and he cut in pieces all the articles of gold*
> *which Solomon king of Israel had made*
> *in the temple of the Lord,*
> *as the Lord had said."*
>
> 2 Kings 24:13

Nothing more is recorded about the 'Ark of the Covenant' and its journey until it is seen again in heaven in the Temple of God. Revelation 11:19

It's All About the Lamb

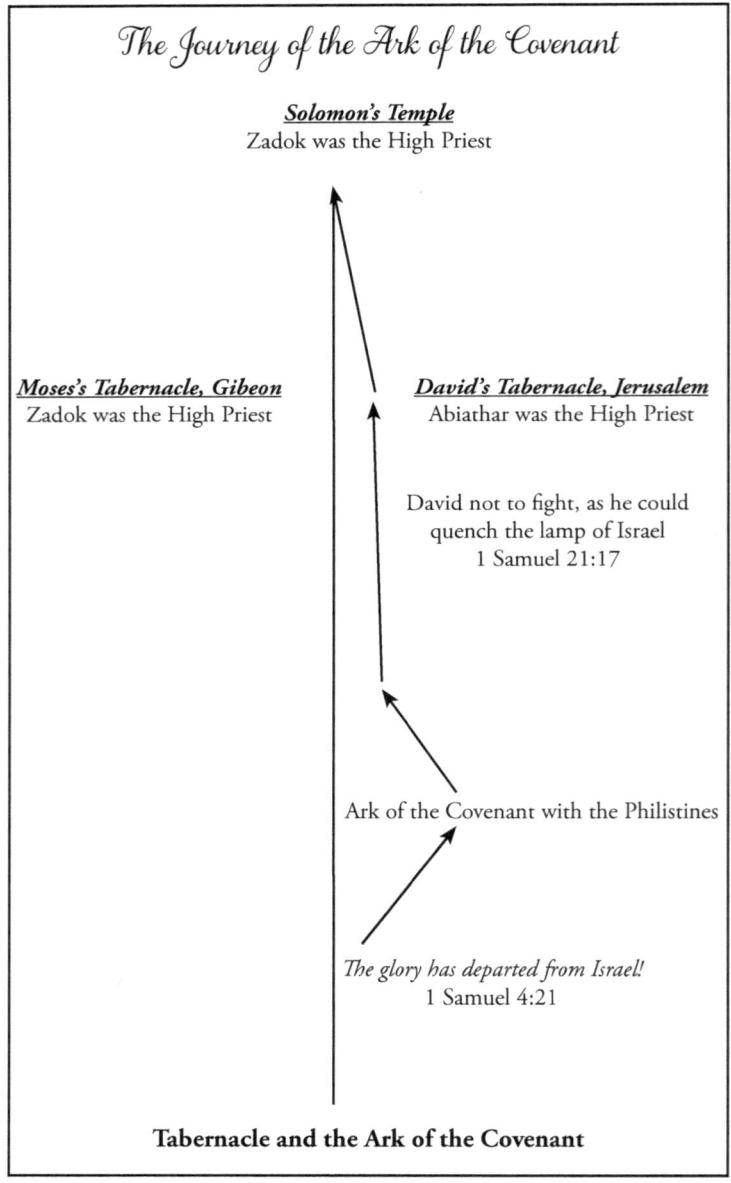

Part 4

It's All About the Lamb

Alpha and Omega

"For My thoughts are not your thoughts,
nor are your ways My ways," says the Lord.
"For as the heavens are higher than the earth,
So are My ways higher than your ways,
and My thoughts than your thoughts."

Isaiah 55:8–9

Father God had a plan for mankind before He created the angels, good and not-so-good, spirits, the heavens and our present world. Father God desired worship, as the beings He created around His throne did not rest day or night but said:

"Holy, Holy, Holy,
Lord God Almighty,
Who was and is and is to come!"

Revelation 4:8b

The Lord spoke, and everything came into existence. When the Spirit of God hovered over the earth and noticed that it was formless and void of any living thing, He created a world to be inhabited by men and women who would worship Him. After He created man and saw that everything was good, He rested.

However, His creatures on earth did not worship the Lord, so the triune God instigated a plan for a specific race of people who would be holy and dedicated to worship Him amongst all the other creatures. So, the Lord formed a man out of the dust of the ground and gave him a special gift not given to any other created being, and that was a soul.

> *"The Lord God planted a garden*
> *eastward in Eden,*
> *and there He put the man*
> *whom He had formed."*
>
> Genesis 2:8

In the Beginning

The Lord God specifically chose a place in Eden where He planted, not created, a garden in the east of Eden. He then placed the man, whom He had formed and also given a soul, in His garden to tend and keep it (Genesis 2:15). Just as Adam was not created, all those other created beings prior to Adam did not have a soul, as this was a unique gift from Father God to Adam and the race that would follow.

Father God gave Adam one commandment to obey, and that was:

> *"Of every tree of the garden you may freely eat;*
> *but of the tree of the knowledge of good and evil*
> *you shall not eat, for in that day that you eat of it*
> *you shall surely die."*

Genesis 2:16a–17

Only after Eve, Adam's God-given wife, had sinned and eaten the forbidden fruit and then gave some to him, which he took and ate, were they both separated from the Lord, as their relationship was broken. The Lord had chosen them both to be His special people reserved to worship Him. He had given them a garden of their own that provided everything they required, even the *'Tree of Life'*, but they chose not to eat of this tree, the other tree in the middle of the Garden of Eden. Genesis 2:9

Adam and Eve were expelled from the Garden to live a different life from the one the Lord had given them. Outside the Garden of Eden, some worshipped the Lord like Abel. Unlike his brother Cain, Abel had a relationship with the Lord where Cain had no understanding. Cain successfully removed the earthly relationship the Lord had with Abel when he killed him.

Others worshipped the Lord, but not as He had commanded. Job had a relationship with Father God. He worshipped the Lord and was a priest to Him, as he made sacrifices daily for his children in case they sinned (Job 1:5). Noah was another who found grace in the eyes of the Lord (Genesis 6:8), but then the Lord destroyed all the inhabitants of the earth except for Noah and his family, whom the Lord kept safe inside the Ark because no others worshipped the Lord.

It was not until Melchizedek met with Abram and renewed the promises previously given (Genesis 12:1a–3) that the promises became a covenant with Abram and his descendants (Genesis 14:19–20). Through the miraculous birth of Isaac to Abraham and Sarah, the covenant seed was born, and the promises were sealed. Would future generations respect and honour the Lord by worshipping Him and obeying His requirements?

A Nation of Priests

The Lord tested various people to see if their faith would trust Him to guide and direct them, grant them protection and blessings. Abraham was asked to sacrifice the promised seed Isaac to the Lord, and because he obediently obeyed the command of the Lord, he was blessed. Eventually, Abraham's descendants lived in the upper part of Canaan, but because of the great famine that took hold of the land, Abraham's descendant Jacob and his families left their home and travelled to Egypt, where Jacob's favourite son, Joseph, was second in charge to Pharaoh.

Jacob's family were eventually known as the Hebrews or the children of Israel, who became a people to be reckoned with as they grew in numbers. When they became slaves to Pharaoh in Egypt, the Lord was training them in discipline, as they were required to obey without question. Eventually, the Lord saw that the Israelites had sufficient training and sent a man by the name of Moses to lead the chosen people of God, the children of Israel, out from under the control of Pharaoh, to bring them under His control.

The children of Israel were part of a mixed culture where many gods were worshipped. Their ancestors had a relationship with the Lord, who provided for their needs through expressed faith. The Hebrews had parted from their ancestral teaching over the years, as a mixed idea of the God of the Israelites was adopted. The people would struggle to adapt as Laws governing their worship and behaviour were introduced.

When the Lord led the children of Israel through the Red Sea and annihilated their oppressors, instead of being thankful and obeying the Lord who had delivered them from slavery, they rebelled continuously. What had happened to the discipline they had learned from all the preceding years? Pride had entered the arena and had taken these Israelites under its control. A people who were supposed to be grateful to the Lord became rebellious, a stiff-necked people who were the chosen people but would always struggle to worship the Lord and His requirement that they should worship Him only, no other gods.

The Israelites would not have reacted to the Egyptians the way they treated the Lord, so what had changed? They didn't understand that in choosing freedom from slavery, they were choosing to obey and honour the Lord out of gratitude for all that He had done. Instead of praising the Lord for His great mercies and recognising his providential care for them, they grumbled and whinged.

The Lord told Moses that He required the Israelites to worship and honour Him. He presented the Ten Commandments to Moses, who shared them with the children of Israel, who accepted the covenant promises laid out for them as a would-be nation.

The first four were all about the Lord and how to worship Him, whereas the other six were about the personal relationship between each other.

You shall have no other gods before Me.

You shall not make idols.

You shall not take the name of the Lord your God in vain.

Remember the Sabbath day, to keep it holy.

Honour your father and your mother.

You shall not murder.

You shall not commit adultery.

You shall not steal.

You shall not bear false witness against your neighbour.

You shall not covet.

Exodus 20:3–17, Deuteronomy 5:7–21

Because the children of Israel could not keep the Law, the Lord, as He did for Adam and Eve, provided a sacrificial system where an animal was slain for the redemption of sins committed. The Tabernacle was made and set up as a place where the Lord's presence could be seen, where the animals were sacrificed to the Lord, and burnt offerings were made.

The Lord also established festive days to be observed, joyous occasions when an extra day of rest or a Sabbath occurred. The seven festive feasts became the 'Feasts of Israel' and are still observed today, but much of the significance and meaning has been lost. The Israelites failed to form a relationship with Father God but developed a spirit of fear and complacency.

About fourteen hundred years would pass, and the people the Lord chose to bring out of slavery faced many trials and difficulties. When the Lord sent a messenger to the people with His Word to turn back to Him and His ways, the people rebelled and grumbled. There was a continual struggle for the Hebrews, who never understood that they could choose between spiritual slavery or servanthood to the Lord or disobedience.

The children of Israel covenanted to be a nation of priests whose whole purpose was to worship the Lord, but because of antagonism, they never came to an understanding, even though many prophets of doom, as they were known, came to guide them in the way the Lord required.

The Law fulfilled the covenant, so keeping the law failed over and over again. When the Lord had enough of the wayward chosen people, He stopped speaking to them for four hundred years, and life continued as it always did. But the children of Israel were unaware and went further into sin without any spiritual guidance from the prophets, as many had been killed for sharing what the Lord had ordained.

The Lord spoke again through an Angel, Gabriel, who appeared next to the 'Incense Altar' set up in Herod's Temple. He waited for Zachariah to reappear from behind the curtain that separated the 'Most Holy Place' from the 'Holy Place' (Luke 1:8–9, v11). The day was Yom Kippur, the most sacred and holy day of the year for the Jews. The angel told him that even though he and his wife were both considered old, his wife Elizabeth would conceive a boy child whom they would call 'John', as he would be the forerunner to the long-awaited Messiah.

Only a few weeks had passed when Gabriel appeared to a young virgin in the town of Nazareth and told her she had found favour with God and would be the mother of the long-awaited Messiah, as the Holy Spirit would come upon her. Although Mary did not understand, she accepted what the angel had prophesied over her. When the time came, Joseph and Mary named the newborn baby Jesus, as He would save His people from their sins.

Father God required man to worship Him of his own free will, but as this did not happen, He chose a group of people, the scribes and the Pharisees, to be His own, disciplined people who would obey the laws He had given to them. Because of man's free will, they again chose to worship themselves and what they wanted instead of worshipping the Lord, except for a remnant.

Father God chose to send His Son, Jesus, to take the place of the sacrificial system, which was the only way to obtain remission for sin. The Lord would choose those whom He knew were prepared to forfeit their free will (John 15:16) and, in obedience, worship the Father, as they gave up all right to their life, to become a slave to the Almighty, to eventually become a kingdom of Priests.

Jesus was born by the Holy Spirit, which meant He was born without the tendency to sin, as sin came through Adam and was inherited by all those born of man. Jesus grew, was baptised and remained the spotless *'Lamb of God'*, as He fulfilled the known will of His Father.

When Jesus had completed His ministry, He met with Moses and Elijah, who agreed with Jesus about the Law and the Prophets (Matthew 5:18), so He was able to complete His sacrificial offering to atone for the sin of mankind, once and for all.

When Jesus was sentenced to death by crucifixion, as He was the unblemished Lamb, His life was acceptable to Father God. Knowing He had completed His earthly task, He said, *"It is finished,"* and as He had the power to lay His life down and was able to take it up again (John 10:18), He yielded up His Spirit to His Father and died.

The Called

Because the sacrificial death of God's Son, Jesus Christ, the Lamb of God, was acceptable, the Holy Spirit was able to inhabit the lives of *'the Called'*. As those chosen yielded their free will to the Lord and became His servants or slaves, because of what Jesus had completed, made those called righteous in the sight of the Lord.

As the promptings of the Holy Spirit were obeyed, forgiveness and guidance were given to show those chosen how to live a life that was pleasing to the Father in thought, word and deed, as a relationship was formed.

While many were called, few are choice (Matthew 22:14), as only those who have ears to hear (Revelation 2:29, 3:6, 13, 22) will be able to comprehend the voice of the Holy Spirit. Two of the Gospel writers retell the parable of *'The Sower'*, and on four different occasions, Jesus refers to people and spiritual hearing. Matthew 11:15, Mark 4:9, Luke 8:8, 14:35.

Jesus, when referring to His return in the Parable of *'The Persistent Widow'*, shared the following verse:

> *"I tell you that He will avenge them speedily.*
> *Nevertheless, when the Son of Man comes,*
> *will He really find faith on the earth?"*

Luke 18:8

Although the Holy Spirit is prompting people to respond, their ears are deaf to the way of Father God. Faith in the Lord to supply all their needs is no longer acceptable, as man is looking to himself and how he can supply his needs. Paul, when writing to Timothy, said the following:

> *"For men will be lovers of themselves,*
> *lovers of money, boasters, proud, blasphemers,*
> *disobedient to parents, unthankful, unholy,*
> *unloving, unforgiving, slanderers, without self-control,*
> *brutal, despisers of good, traitors, headstrong, haughty,*
> *lovers of pleasure rather than lover of God,*
> *having a form of godliness but denying its power."*
>
> 2 Timothy 3:2–5a

Father God has given man every resource available to be part of His chosen people to worship Him in spirit and in truth (John 4:23–24). While we can understand 'spirit' as Father God is a Spirit and we are a spirit, as God is Truth (John 14:6), and the Holy Spirit will guide us into all truth (John 16:13), Jesus said that the *"Truth shall make you free"* (John 8:32), so what is truth?

Prompted to search the Psalms, I would share the following verses:

> *"How can a young man cleanse his ways?*
> *By taking heed to Your word.*
> *With my whole heart I have sought You;*
> *Oh, let me not wander from Your commandments!*
> *Your word I have hidden in my heart,*
> *that I might not sin against You."*
>
> Psalm 119:9–11

The psalmist said, *"Your word I have hidden in my heart."* The truth is hidden in our heart, so what is referred to as the heart?

> *"And the Lord God formed man*
> *of the dust of the ground,*
> *and breathed into his nostrils*
> *the breath of life;*
> *and man became a living soul."*
>
> Genesis 2:7

God took a spirit and clothed it in the dust of the earth, formed a man and gave him a soul. As we meditate on what the Holy Spirit enables us to understand, we store them up in our soul. Jesus gave fair warning about not doing this when He said:

> *"Do not fear those who kill the body*
> *but cannot kill the soul.*
> *But rather fear Him who is able*
> *to destroy both soul and body in hell."*
>
> Matthew 10:28

To say that God is truth is to acknowledge that truth itself proceeds from the nature of God. While many things can have the truth, only one thing can be the truth, with that one thing being God Himself. The Hebrew term for *'truth'* is 'emet', which means 'truth', 'firmness', 'stability', and 'faithfulness'. True worship of Father God must come from the soul He gave us, as anything else is unacceptable and will be destroyed on the last day along with our new body.

The Lord Jesus Christ gave us three warning signs to be aware of as to how the return of Jesus would happen. *"Like a flash of lightning"* (Matthew 24:27), *"In the twinkling of an eye"* (1 Corinthians 15:52), and *"Like a thief in the night"* (1 Thessalonians 5:2). The psalmist referred to His return when he wrote:

> *"The nations raged,*
> *the kingdoms were moved;*
> *He uttered His voice,*
> *the earth melted."*
>
> Psalm 46:6

When the Lord's time is right, just as He spoke everything into existence, so He will speak everything out of existence. In a moment, time will cease to exist as our spirit and soul will see Jesus coming to gather His own. That will be a glorious occasion for all those who are washed in the *'Blood of the Lamb'*. Just as the shepherd knows his own sheep by name and leads them out (John 10:3), so each of *'the Called'* will gather with the *'Good Shepherd'*.

Father God will then dispatch those who have not accepted the *'Blood of the Lamb'* to the lake burning with fire and brimstone to accompany the devil and his angels for all eternity, after they have bowed before Jesus and acknowledged Him as Lord. The sheep and the goats will then be sorted, just as Gideon was able to choose 'the called' who the Lord required to fulfil His will.

Thirty-two thousand souls who thought they were entitled to fight the spiritual battle were reduced to three hundred. What should this tell us about the final judgement? Those who are selected as goats will then join those who have already received their reward in the lake of fire.

As our spirit and soul have received our new body, all things have passed away, and everything has become new. A new heaven and a new earth, a new Jerusalem where we will be shown our place that Jesus has reserved just for us as we obediently worship Father God for all eternity. The Father will finally have His kingdom of faithful priests who only want to worship Him for eternity.

For those who have a discerning eye, the overall plan of Father God was demonstrated by Joseph when he chose to care for Mary and her baby, as Joseph was responsible for Jesus and His earthly upbringing.

When Mary told Joseph she was pregnant, he did not know what to do. Mary being pregnant in this time of betrothal was not something Joseph found easy to accept. He thought it was best to break off the engagement. But an angel visited Joseph and assured him the pregnancy was the will of God, and he was to marry Mary (Matthew 1:18–25). Joseph was obedient to the known will of God and eventually married his betrothed wife, but not until she had brought forth that which was Holy to the Lord. Luke 2:5–7

As the account of Joseph and his decision-making is read, it appeared he had three courses of action.

Firstly, he could break off the engagement and make Mary a very public spectacle. This would lay the complete blame at the feet of Mary, and she would be found guilty of adultery. She would be humiliated in front of all those who knew her, including her parents, which would have brought disgrace to the family. Then, she would have been stoned to death.

Joseph was a 'Just Man', and his reasoning about Mary's condition demonstrated his maturity. As their marriage could have been arranged, Joseph may have been some years older than Mary, as his mature response showed the love he had for his betrothed bride, Mary.

Joseph was within his right to divorce Mary according to Levitical law, *"When a man takes a wife and marries her, and he finds some uncleanness in her, he can write a certificate of divorce, put it in her hand and send her out of his house"* (Deuteronomy 24:1). Joseph could have thought Mary's pregnancy as being unclean because the child was conceived out of wedlock, but because the conception was by the Holy Spirit, no contamination or blemish was present in any way, shape or form.

Secondly, Joseph could put her away quietly (Matthew 1:19). This meant Joseph would share the responsibility with Mary as no public spectacle would be made, but she would live and have the baby without Joseph's support.

Thirdly, choosing to marry Mary meant Joseph would accept full responsibility for Mary and her baby, even though he had committed no sin and was not the father of the child. Such was his love for his betrothed; Joseph did not hesitate to obey the command of God, delivered by the angel.

There is a great underlying lesson in Joseph's response to Mary's situation. Just as Joseph accepted full responsibility for Mary's condition and covered the situation of his betrothed wife-to-be, Jesus accepted full responsibility for our sin. I see Joseph is so much like Jesus.

Jesus could have taken the first option to let the world and the people within die in their sins. But He didn't. Jesus could have compelled people to share the responsibility for their sins by keeping the Law, which was the second option. But He didn't.

Jesus chose to die for our sins, taking full responsibility for our sins. The love that Father God has for us, His children, through Jesus is giving us life, whereas we deserve death.

When Father God declares all things are ready, Jesus will return to claim His bride, the Church. Although the Church is mostly unfaithful to Him, there is a remnant within the church that has remained faithful. This aligns with the teaching about the sheep and goats (Matthew 25:31–46). The main body of the church is represented by goats, the remnant as sheep. Mary was a favoured one.

Jesus, in His teaching, said, *"Many are called but few are choice"* (Matthew 22:14). While many were called to be the children of Israel, Mary was a choice one, called to a special task by God. Mary was part of the remnant. When Jesus returns to usher His own into eternity, the sins of the remnant are covered by the shed blood of Jesus. Even though He was without sin, *"He made Him who knew no sin to be sin for us, that we might become the righteousness of God in Him"* (2 Corinthians 5:21).

> *"Now to Him who is able to keep*
> *you from stumbling,*
> *and to present you faultless*
> *before the presence of His glory*
> *with exceeding joy,*
> *to God our Saviour,*
> *Who alone is wise,*

> *be glory and majesty, dominion and power,*
> *both now and forever. Amen."*
>
> Jude 24–25

Conclusion

Father God requires us to worship Him! The question now posed is, "What is worship?"

Worship is when we give our deepest affection and highest praise to God. True worship of God is when we love Him with all our heart, soul, mind, and strength. True worship is when we prize God above everything else and put Him first in our heart. True worship is all about a relationship. Deuteronomy 6:4–5

Our soul is the most prized possession we have been given, yet many are like Esau, who sell their birthright, their soul, for the passing pleasures of life (Genesis 25:31–34). Jesus shared the following teaching about our soul when He said:

> *"For what will it profit a man*
> *if he gains the whole world,*
> *and loses his own soul.*
> *Or what will a man give*
> *in exchange for his soul?"*
>
> Mark 8:36–37

What Jesus is saying is that if we sell everything to gain the world, the world is not enough to buy back our soul. The world is not enough! Satan's main aim is to destroy the soul of a man, as when the soul is destroyed, we have nothing to give Father God on the day of reckoning. Nothing else is required but a soul that is rich in the things of God, not devastated with the things of earth.

Scripture outlined very clearly that the condition of the soul is to be prized and protected at all costs. The psalmist recorded the following verses when he said:

> *"Give to the Lord the glory due His name;*
> *Bring an offering, and come into His courts.*
> *Oh, worship the Lord in the beauty of holiness!*
> *Tremble before Him, all the earth."*
>
> Psalm 96:8–9

The Psalmist says, *"Oh, worship the Lord in the beauty of holiness!"* Holiness is defined as obedience to the known will of God as He reveals Himself to your own heart. Once we have tested what has been given to us and know for certain the instructions have come from the Father, then complete obedience is the only course of action for us to take.

To illustrate what has been written, I am prompted to share the proceedings of the wedding at Canna of Galilee. (John 2:1–11). Mary came to Jesus and told Him they had run out of wine.

She told the servants to do whatever Jesus said. The servants obeyed Jesus' instructions and took the wine to the master of the feast, who praised the wine as the best.

How many were involved in this miracle? Jesus, Mary, servants, master of the feast and the hosts. There were at least seven involved in this event. The question is, who benefited from the miracle? The answer is the hosts, as they were not embarrassed. So, how does this involve holiness? The answer is all about who gets the glory and praise. I see the master of the feast as Father God. Mary is the prompting of the Holy Spirit, and Jesus is Jesus. The servants are you and me, while the hosts are the remnant.

Did you notice the servants did not question what they were asked to do? They obediently carried out the known will of Jesus as He revealed His thoughts to them. The servants may have wondered what Jesus was doing, but they obeyed completely. The outcome was that the master of the feast received the glory and thanks due, and all the others were blessed, not embarrassed.

Only when a true relationship between Father God and His chosen people is in place can a person truly worship the One who has given them life, not death. The Israelites were not grateful to the Father for delivering them from death to life but took on the expectation that God owed them and were full of pride. This situation happened when Satan was thrown out of heaven because of pride issues. Revelation 12:7–9

The reversal will happen when the chosen are called to be one with the Father to worship Him. Because of our relationship with Father God, in response to what Jesus accomplished, the promptings from the Holy Spirit obeyed, we will exhibit thankfulness, gratitude, and praise as we continue in this state for eternity because, in this Passover, we have passed over from death to life. It's all about our relationship with the Father.

True worship is never questioning a direct prompting from the Holy Spirit but in obedience, carrying out the prescribed instructions correctly, not with any modification. Complete obedience to the known will of God is the only acceptable correct application to His revealed will.

To maintain a right spirit within ourselves, it is always good to remember the prayer David prayed when he said:

> *"Create in me a clean heart, O God,*
> *and renew a right spirit within me."*
>
> Psalm 51:10a

Paul, when writing to the Philippians, gave them sound advice as to how to keep a right spirit and their soul clean unto the Lord when he said:

> *"Whatever things are true,*
> *whatever things are notable,*
> *whatever things are just,*

> *whatever things are pure,*
> *whatever things are lovely,*
> *whatever things are of a good report,*
> *if there is any virtue*
> *and if there is anything praiseworthy,*
> *meditate on these things."*
>
> Philippians 3:8

Paul also had some wise words for the Romans when he wrote:

> *"Do not be conformed to the world,*
> *but be transformed by the renewing of your mind,*
> *that you may prove what is that good*
> *and acceptable and perfect will of God."*
>
> Romans 12:2

Worship to Father God is all about the purity of our soul because our soul determines what the spirit does. On the day of judgement, the question Father God will ask us is, "What have you done with the soul I breathed into you?" Will He take the sword of the Spirit and cut away all the bad to reveal the true essence of your soul, or will He say:

> *"Well done, good and faithful servant;*
> *you have been faithful over a few things,*
> *I will make you a ruler over many things,*
> *enter into the joy of your Lord."*

Matthew 25:23

Always remember the words of Mary to our Lord when she said:

> *"Whatever He says,*
> *do it!"*

John 2:5b

> *"He who testifies to these things says,*
> *'Surely I am coming quickly.' Amen.*
> *Even so, come, Lord Jesus!*
> *The grace of our Lord Jesus Christ*
> *be with you all. Amen."*

Revelation 22:20–21

"The Shaking"

A poem about the End Times
by Dr. Richard Booker, July 12, 2016

Things that are must come to an end,
Before things that are better can begin.

*

In time of trouble, will you stand or bend,
Fear not the future for God is a faithful friend.

*

Everything we know is about to change,
But God's not nervous, He's forever the same.

*

The world as we know it is coming to an end,
But God has a plan, His kingdom is at hand.

*

So, pray as a watchman awake and alert,
Love one another and cause no hurt.

*

"The Shaking"

Serve those around you without pretence,
Minister in the Spirit and don't take offence.
*

For soon we will hear the shofar blown,
Jesus is coming and it won't be long.
*

The Lion of Judah, Yeshua is His name,
To make us one with the Father is the reason He came.
*

So, let's all get ready for the coming of the King,
The glory of God He is returning to bring.
*

Used by permission of the author

Other Books by the Author

Available from www.wittonbooks.com

The Path of Life focuses on the three promises God gave to Abram. While some ancestry is used, the main story is contained within the life of Moses and his successor, Joshua. An in-depth study of God's dealing with and shaping of the children of Israel through Moses provides much thought-provoking reading and revelation that has never been taught.

Betrayal can be found anywhere. It is not confined to two people. Family, friends, work colleagues, recreational groups, and the church. Betrayal manifests itself wherever two or three are gathered.

Seven characters from the Old Testament are featured to show 'Betrayal' as the force that cost them their life or made them spiritually stronger.

Abel, Noah, Job, Joseph, Gideon, Samson, David, Jesus, and Judas are included.

As each of their lives is studied, in the main, one thing that never suffered defeat was their love for Father God. In return, He provided all they needed including protection from the evil forces. Judas was the exception.

Available from www.wittonbooks.com

Have you ever searched the four gospels to obtain the full account of Jesus' life?

The author, under the guidance of the Holy Spirit, took the words of the Apostle Paul to heart, when the latter wrote to Timothy and encouraged him to "Study to show yourself approved unto God, a workman that needs not be ashamed, rightly dividing the word of truth."

2 Timothy 2:15

In *The Life of Jesus: A Simple Narrative* the author uses language similar to the New King James Version of the Bible to order and blend the four gospels into one complete story.

In the second book, *The Life of Christ Simply Told*, the author uses language similar to the New International Version of the Bible to order and blend the four gospels into the complete story of Jesus' life.

Available from www.wittonbooks.com

God, Man, Lucifer and the End Time contains a collection of seven stand-alone documents. However, they all overlap and combine in a way only the Holy Spirit could implement. They are complex topics, requiring a great deal of study to 'bring it together'.

Prompted by the Holy Spirit and this work used as the 'foundation', may it lead to a greater understanding of the truth, majesty and love of our God.

Life's a Journey introduces the reader to the roads taken by several Bible characters and the consequences of their chosen walks. Those introduced are Mary, John the Baptist, Andrew, John the Disciple, and the children of Israel.

A second section brings a light-hearted twist, as the author shares real-life incidents, although the setting has been changed to add further humour to the already hilarious accounts of his eventful life.

Each of us has a journey to walk. Some long, some short, and some heart-breaking, others blessed. May each who reads glean encouragement for your life's walk.

Available from www.wittonbooks.com
and *The Adventures of Max* Facebook page

Series titles available:

Book 1	*The Defiant Mouse*
Book 2	*The Curious Chicken*
Book 3	*A Dog in Need*
Book 4	*An Old Friend Found*
Book 5	*The Rescue*
Book 6	*The Bush Fire*
Book 7	*A Bad Influence*
Book 8	*A Shining Light*
Book 9	*Hidden Secrets*
Book 10	*A Foiled Plot*
Book 11	*Running the Race*
Book 12	*An Unexpected Reward*
Book 13	*Max Meets a Friend*
Book 14	*Reflections*

**Available from www.wittonbooks.com
and *Manuel's Missions* Facebook page**

Series titles available:

Book 1	*The Servant Mouse*
Book 2	*A Cherished Place*
Book 3	*Manuel and the Spider*
Book 4	*A Generous Giver*
Book 5	*Lost and Found*
Book 6	*Manuel's Day Out*
Book 7	*Love One Another*
Book 8	*Observations*

Available from www.wittonbooks.com

After attending a pre-Christmas church eveing, I came away feeling numb due to the presentation of the Christmas story, by very secular people.

As you read, my prayer is that the Holy spirit will not only impart wisdom, but a deep understanding of the real Nativity story.

Available from www.wittonbooks.com

It's All About the Lamb explores the way the Passover, the Tabernacle and the Ark of the Covenant foreshadow Jesus' ministry. Jesus is the thread that runs through the Bible — often concealed in Scripture and even hidden in Hebrew practices and artefacts.

Protection, liberation, training and celebration are all connected through these powerful 'types' to serve as an everlasting reminder of the saving role of Jesus, our Great High Priest. Today, we have His presence within us. And all this has been achieved through the Lamb of God, who came to set us free.

www.ingramcontent.com/pod-product-compliance
Lightning Source LLC
Chambersburg PA
CBHW062033290426
44109CB00026B/2620